So You've Got Your Real Estate License...

NOW WHAT?

Mitch Ribak

MITCH RIBAK

SO YOU'VE GOT YOUR REAL ESTATE LICENSE

Another Fine Edit by www.awriterforlife.com

Edited by Jaimie M. Engle

Copyright © 2015 Mitch Ribak
All Rights Reserved
Published by 100 MPH Publishing
First edition paperback printed May 2015
Printed in the United States of America
Cover Design and Layout by Philip Benjamin

ISBN-13: 978-0692456316
ISBN-10: 0692456317

MITCH RIBAK

Dedication

I want to dedicate this book to my awesome, patient wife, my Real Estate Agents and all the Realtors who have been following my systems for almost 10 years!

Acknowledgments

This book couldn't have happened without the help and inspiration of many people. First, of course, is my beautiful wife who puts up with all my crazy aspirations; also my editor, Jaimie M. Engle, who constantly hounded me to get my chapters to her; finally, I would like to mention that without my Agents and my staff I would never have been able to test all my theories for your benefit!

Trial and Error is awesome….sometimes!

Table of Contents

So you've decided to become a Realtor!

You know the advantages – the low cost of starting up, the potential to make lots of money and to be your own boss. These well-known advantages lure you in, but the little known and less discussed pitfalls may wash you out.

You'll need to be aware of the pitfalls that may pose obstacles to your success. Once those are out of your way, the sky is the limit for profitable professional growth and enjoyment in the real estate industry.

The author, Mitch Ribak will take you through the pitfalls and show you how to avoid them. Then he will teach you how to succeed as a Realtor.

This book is part how to and part inspiration. It's written in a chatty breezy style that intersperses personal and riveting anecdotes taken from his life and real estate career. The book is no less profound for having been written in such a narrative form. Mitch writes as he speaks. When Mitch speaks people listen, when he writes they listen too! And when they listen, they learn.

From this book, you'll learn basic principles and specific proven tactics on being a successful Realtor. You'll learn the importance of referrals and how to get them. You'll learn that helping is selling. You'll learn how to educate your clients, the mechanics of a home sale, how to represent buyers or sellers, organization, time management, winning phone techniques for a variety of circumstances, how to use technology to your advantage, how to network, the power of free and

National Pizza Day, the importance of leads and how to generate them online and offline and how to cultivate them.

You will learn!

You will also be inspired. As you devour these pages, you will be inspired by Mitch's indomitable spirit, his work ethic, his success, his honesty, his integrity, his desire to help, his "must list" and his life story that includes two near death experiences.

Mitch also shares with you client form letters and his systems –the actual work product he uses in his own real estate brokerage, Tropical Reality of Suntree.

As you read, you'll realize Mitch is helping you by selling you on his system.

I've worked with Mitch for over a decade helping him with traffic acquisition and web site conversion first as the General Manager of HomeGain, a real estate portal and most recently as a real estate consultant at Smaulgld.com. Mitch's commitment to helping is immense, but it's his life learned skills and insights that give him his priceless *ability* to help.

Here is a book spoiler alert: Honesty + Ethics + Desire to Help = Success

How can it be that simple? It's not. As Mitch writes "it doesn't mean it is *easy* to get started"

Enough! You've got the book, now Just Read it, then Just Do it!

Louis Cammarosano
owner www.smaugld.com

Chapter One: Understanding What You Got Yourself Into!

I have met so many Realtors with the same misconception that being a Realtor is this glamorous way to earn a living. There are some awesome aspects of being a Realtor, such as flexible time, the ability to get involved in the community and, my favorite, the ability to run your own business for a very minimal investment.

Here is the reality, which to me, is the most important aspect of your new venture: being a Realtor is a business. It's a tough business that requires full time work of at least 40-50 hours per week or more. Just think about it, if you invested $100,000 in a business, what would you do to succeed at your business? If you are like most people, you would do almost anything. However, when investing usually no more than $1500 - $2000, the "hurt" of losing the investment to an Agent isn't so bad. After all, we have all wasted a couple grand here and there.

So what does it mean to run your Real Estate career as a business? It means that to be successful, you have to implement systems and follow those systems to your future. To run a successful business you have to start with a plan. The contents of this book are going to touch on several subjects such as basic sales, evaluating your customers, maximizing floor time, understanding your numbers and, most importantly, understanding how to generate leads and convert those leads (regardless of how you get them) into customers for life.

One of the best experiences of my Real Estate Career has been being President of our local Realtor Association, Space Coast Association of Realtors, for 2014. Obviously there are many benefits, but the best benefit is having almost every Realtor in the county know who I am and the name of my company. Here are some stats from my local board for 2013. Only 168 Agents out of 3,000 did over $4 million in business which equates to approximately $75k-$100k or so depending on your split. Only 1,000 did over $1 million in business which equates to $15k - $25k or so depending on your split. 2,000 Agents made less than $15k in 2012. Basically, just a small percent of those involved in Real Estate generate a high income. Your income, of course, will depend on where you live and the cost of housing in your area. The average price range in Brevard County, where my company is located is $130,000. We have to sell a lot of homes to make a living.

Now the good news: if you implement even just a few things from this book, you will be in the top 5% of the Realtors in your area. Success in this business has nothing to do with luck (ok, just a little bit) and everything to do with work ethic, systems and a good business plan. During the downturn from 2006-2011, my brokerage grew 10%-20% each year while other brokerages were falling apart. The reason? We had good systems, good training and, most of all, a good plan! Follow my plans throughout this book and you will find success. Every agent in my office, who actually follows what I teach, does very well.

So why do agents fail? There are several reasons I want to touch on. The purpose for this section isn't to depress you, it's to get you to understand that your mindset will determine your future in this business:

1) <u>Independent Contractor</u> - To me this is huge. If I had to do my Brokerage all over again, I would make everyone an employee. As a Broker, I can't dictate to any of my Agents that they need to do anything. It's up to them to actually be self-motivated and as a Broker I have to hope you actually work. Employees have to work or they will be replaced.

2) <u>Change in career</u> - I like to use a couple of examples with regard to those of you who had a regular job for 10, 20, or 30 years. For most of you, you have worked a 9-5 job for the past   so many years. You went to work at 9am, completed the work you had to get done on your desk, and then went home at the end of the day. Your weekends were filled with family, fun and doing stuff around the house. All of a sudden you become a Realtor and there is nobody to report to. You don't have to be at the office at 9am. You don't have someone giving you daily work to accomplish. All of a sudden, you have this new found freedom! You are officially on your own. Unfortunately, most Agents will take advantage of this by sleeping in, starting their workday around 10am, and working till 2pm. Then they try to figure out why they aren't making any money.

The other way I like to look at this is our school years. You spent 12 years (more if you went to kindergarten) following a structure. You woke up, went to school, got home, did homework, ate dinner and went to bed to start over again the next day. Okay. I know it wasn't always in that order, but you get the idea. Now, you graduate high school and you go to college as a freshman. All of a sudden you don't have to wake up early and go to class if you don't want too. You don't have to do homework if you don't want too. You can stay up as late as you want, even all night, if you want too. All of a sudden you have a freedom that you have never had before. Never mind all the outside influences that we have all seen in college. This is the reason most kids fail or do terrible during their freshman year. It takes them a full year to realize freedom is not to be taken lightly.

New Agents always run the risk of failing right from the start. All the odds are against you. Only you can determine if you are going to be successful or not.

3) <u>Mindset</u> - This is another huge aspect of whether you will be successful or not. Those who do not have positive mindsets and attitudes will most likely fail miserably in this business. It's not that successful Agents don't have bad days; they do. But they know how to compartmentalize those moments so they don't affect their daily work. I'm going to tell you a little story (which I'll do a lot throughout the book) about how powerful mindset is and how it can change any outcome in your life.

*   *   *

The year was 1978. Back then I played guitar in a rock band and had as good a time as a teenager could have. We played throughout New England and were booked pretty much every Friday and Saturday each week. I graduated high school in 1978 (yes, I'm old, but it's only a number) and our band was doing great. We had a huge gig planned in a few weeks playing to a sold out crowd in an area where we had our biggest fan base. It was the first show that we not only played, but set up and promoted. This was big for us!

My friends and I pulled into a gas station to get some gas. It was August 22nd at 7:45pm, a Mobil station. The events that happened next are never too far from my mind. This was way before self-serve gas stations. The attendant was busy and had other cars to deal with, so I jumped out of the car and pumped the gas. While pumping, the tank spit back at me, and I got about a six inch circle of gas on the nylon fishnet shirt I was wearing. I didn't think anything of it. I went back in the car and one of my friends who was sitting next to me asked for a light for his cigarette. I clicked my lighter and my shirt, and myself, went up in flames. The fumes from the gas on my shirt had ignited. Luckily my friend remembered "drop and roll" that Jerry Lewis used to talk about on television. He pulled me from the car, burning his hands, and threw me to the ground. At that point, in a short time, he put out the fire.

While I was on fire it was an interesting time. According to my friends I was outwardly screaming. I don't remember that. I do remember rolling one way and seeing the gas station gas tanks, and then rolling the other way and seeing the car gas tank. I was thinking how my friends needed to get out of there because everything was going to blow up. I also thought about my parents and was worried my dad would have a heart attack when he found out I died. I was very calm inside and there was no pain. From what I have been told it's the acceptance part before you die.

All of a sudden the fire was put out and I was brought back to reality very quickly. I had third degree burns over 20% of my body. I was burned from my chest all the way down to the bottom of my stomach. The pain was incredible. It's the worst pain I have ever felt in my life and I hope never to feel anything like that again. It was horrible.

The ambulance poured 10 gallons of ice water over me on the way to the hospital. They had to get my 106° temperature down. When I got to the hospital it was frantic, with doctors and nurses working on me. I remember it pretty clearly, for being 35 years ago. Like I said, it's something you don't forget. When they finally stabilized me 6 hours later and got me into intensive care, the doctors were talking with my parents by my bedside. They told them that if I was on fire for 10 seconds more I would have died. The fire would have burned into my organs. On my left hand you could see bone. My other hand was badly burned and my arms, chest and stomach were a mess. The doctors also told my parents that for burns this severe, I would be in the hospital from 4-6 months to recover.

As you can imagine this was pretty traumatic for my parents, my friends and especially for a happy kid like me who played guitar and baseball. My hands were pretty important to me!

Two days later I was moved out of intensive care and my doctor came in to see me. He explained what I was going to go through to recover and talked about possible skin grafts. But most importantly he said that once I could squeeze my hands into a fist, I would be able to leave. I now had a goal!

The band continued to play with a replacement guitarist (who was much better than me) and I was not happy about that. Our gig was just a little more than two weeks away and I did not want to miss it. Every morning I was taken down to the whirlpool set at 105° where they would take all the dead skin off me. Every day I would spend my time listening to 8 track tapes, visiting with friends and eating. The nurses were awesome and the morphine kept me smiling! Nighttime was a different story. I would sit in my bed, tears coming down my face, as I spent hours trying to make a fist. As the new skin continued to grow on my hands, I had to stretch it to make my hands usable again. It was painful, but I had a goal.

Over the next week my doctors were amazed at how quickly I was recovering. I still remember the day the doctor came into my room. It was a Tuesday morning, and I sat there with a big smile on my face opening and closing my fists. I was discharged from the hospital later that day. I didn't know the answer until 35 years later, but obviously something was driving me to get out of that hospital besides wanting to play that gig.

I was out of the hospital in just two-and-a-half weeks. I went from almost dying to playing at my gig 3 weeks later to the day. Other doctors from hospitals all over the state and country came to visit me as there was no medical reason why I was doing so well. How did I accomplish this? It was mindset.

So as you embark on your Real Estate career or if you are trying to get a jumpstart in your career, remember your mindset will determine your outcome.

A truly honest positive mindset will help you overcome hurdles you never thought possible before. One of my favorite quotes is by Henry Ford: "Whether you think you can or think you can't, you are right." If you believe that you can become successful in Real Estate, then you most certainly can. If you have doubts, you will struggle. Get in the mindset and change your life!

4) Systems - One of the books I recommend any budding entrepreneur read is *eMyth Revisited* by Michael Gerber. It's a great book about understanding systems and documenting your processes. It's so important to have a procedure in every aspect of your business. In this book you will see how I have a system for just about every aspect of my business. I have a purpose for everything I do. If you don't have systems, it's a tough business to thrive in. We will discuss everything from Floor Calls to FSBOs to Offline Marketing to Online Marketing and everything in between. Each program I discuss will help you develop your own systems (or follow mine) to help you grow your business.

5) Choosing the wrong Brokerage - To me this could be your biggest downfall. Most Brokers are not meant to be mentors, teachers, or even advisors when it comes to Real Estate. The Brokerage you choose can make or break you in this business. Here is the reality, most Brokers become Brokers so they can continue to work their own business while hopefully earning a few bucks off of the Agents they can bring on board with them. In essence, it is a way for them to earn 100% commissions on the properties they sell. Most Brokers are competing

Brokers. It took me awhile to realize how much my decision to joining the right or wrong Brokerage affected the outcome.

So what is right and what is wrong? Well this depends on you. The hardest part of getting started in this business is your ability to generate business. Most Realtors have no clue how to market themselves, network themselves or generate a constant stream of leads. So here are a few things for new or struggling Realtors to look at when deciding on a Brokerage to join.

i) *Join a Brokerage with a good lead system* - These days many Brokerages are generating leads through the Internet to help support their Agents. I have built my entire Brokerage from Internet leads. However, if you are going to join a Brokerage like this, be sure they have the proper tools in place to help convert those leads to sales. In the end, if you are afraid of the phone, you will most likely struggle in a lead-driven system. In reality, if you are afraid of the phone, you are probably in the wrong business. We will talk about that in a minute.

ii) *Join a Brokerage based on what they offer, not commission splits* - I have interviewed so many Agents that believe they need to get a 70% or higher commission split from day one. The truth is, you can have 100% commission split, but if you don't have the right tools and training, you won't succeed. For instance, if you join a Brokerage with a good lead system, you can expect to get around a 50% commission split. My Brokerage offers a 50% split with our lead system. There have been many Agents I would have hired but they felt they should receive a higher split. Most of these Agents are not in the business anymore.

iii) *Join a Brokerage that offers great in-house training* - Just because a Brokerage has a lot of online training tools doesn't guarantee that you will have proper training. Training should include sales, contract, showings, evaluating the customer, sales strategy and so much more. If a Brokerage offers you great hands-on training, your potential for success is highly elevated.

6) <u>Lack of Sales Training and Ability</u> - Being a Realtor is a sales position. I have heard many Realtors over the years tell me they don't think being a Realtor is being a salesperson. Unfortunately, most of those Realtors are no longer Realtors.

To be successful in Real Estate, you have to understand the basics of sales. The most important aspect of sales in Real Estate is prospecting and the most successful Agents in the business prospect daily. If you read any sales book, and I recommend you read many, there will be one consistent message: you must prospect 2-3 hours per day to be successful in ANY sales position. It's universal!

Let's look at my top Agent this year, Ned, and my worse Agent. (I won't mention his name as I'm going to make him read this book!) What is the difference between the two Agents? Firstly, Ned is one of the most genuine persons you would ever meet. As soon as you talk to him, you know right away that his main goal is to help you accomplish your goals. He is there to help you. We will discuss the Help/Sell philosophy later in this book. My other Agent—we will call him Joe—is a good guy, but you don't get that warm feeling when you talk with him. A consumer might get the wrong feeling about Joe's agenda. With Ned, you know his agenda...it's to help you.

Regardless of their agendas, there is one main difference between the two. When Ned isn't showing property, he is constantly on the phone calling his leads and his customers. He knows that the more he "prospects" his database, the greater his chance to make a connection. It also builds a relationship that far exceeds the initial transaction. Most of Ned's business comes from our lead system. Because of Ned's constant communication, he now receives more than 50% of his business from past customers and referrals.

Joe, on the other hand, barely makes calls. He spends maybe an hour a month calling new leads and seldom, if ever, follows up on leads. Like I said, he is a good guy, but he doesn't build relationships with his leads, and therefore, has really failed in the business. If Joe would adopt Ned's communication and calling habits, Joe could be equally as successful.

This all comes down to sales training. Understanding how to follow up and contact your customers, both new and old, needs to be your priority in business. I'll give you another example.

Walter has had his license for one month. In his first month, he wrote 5 offers, 3 contracts and 1 listing from his circle of influence. He is on the phone constantly and makes things happen. If you can't do this, you will have mediocre success in this business. There is a reason why 95% of Realtors don't earn a good living selling homes. Walter had the same training and tools as any of my other Agents, but Walter has a stronger work ethic than most and understands the importance of sales and prospecting.

7) <u>Lack of Work Ethic</u> – Okay, so ask yourself this: why did you get in this business? Did you get in this business because you thought it was going to be fun to be a Realtor? Or did you get in this business because you really wanted to succeed? To succeed in this business, you need to have a strong disciplined work ethic. It's vital to your success and without it, you won't make it.

   To do this you need to have structure in your life. One of my top Agents structures her day as follows:

   a) Wake up, have some coffee and answer emails - 7am - 8am
   b) 8am - 10am - Call leads from database and call past customers
   c) 10am - 11am - Answer more emails and follow up phone calls on transactions in process
   d) 11am - noon - Prepare for afternoon showings
   e) noon - 1pm - Take a lunch break
   f) 1pm - 5pm - Show property (if not showing property, back on the phone calling database)
   g) 5pm- 6pm - Plan the next day activities

This is her typical day. Yes, things do change based on different circumstances, but most days, you can see she is very organized and has a purpose. You should be spending 80% of your day working on revenue generating activities.

If you are looking at this as a business, as you should be, keep the mindset that you invested $100,000 instead of the $2,000 you actually spent to start your Real Estate career. Think about it; if you invested $100,000 of your hard earned money, what would you do to build your business? Would you work 8 hours per day, 10 hours per day, 12 hours per day? My guess is you would work extremely hard if you invested a ton of money. Lack of work ethic is related to the lack of investment in your business.

8. Lack of Time Management – Sometimes, I feel like a broken record (or a disc for those who don't remember records). Once you begin your career and you start actually getting busy, it will be mandatory to manage your time efficiently. As you can see by the daily schedule of one of my top Agents, she is very structured in her day. I once had all my Agents, including myself, keep a time sheet of everything they did over a 7 day period. Once compiled, they were amazed to see that even though they thought they were working hard, they were only working an average of 4-5 hours per day. At the time, I was working 16 hour days and because of this exercise, it showed me I was only working on revenue generating activities for 10 hours per days. I adjusted my work process immediately and now only work 12 hour days and accomplish more.

Adopting a good Time Management program is not hard. I'll get into the program in detail later in this book. Start thinking about your day and how you go about every minute of your day. How much time do you waste? Follow the exercise I did with my Agents to get a true picture of your day and the areas you spend more time than you should. You will quickly see how having a strong time management plan will equate to accomplishing your goals.

9. <u>No Written Goals and Action Plans</u> - How can you accomplish success without having written goals and a plan of action to accomplish those goals? The answer is simple, you can't! In order for any business to succeed, they must have a business plan that is written, easy to follow and realistic. Each year, at the end of December, I write down what I want to accomplish the following year. I look at my past year and see what I was able to accomplish and what I couldn't accomplish. I question why I failed at a few of my goals. The main reason is I almost always bite off more than I can chew. Yes, even I'm not perfect at all this stuff! Most Realtors who fail in business fail to write down their goals and keep them realistic. Many just pick an arbitrary number such as 36 or 48 sales but they don't have any idea how they will reach that goal. They have no plan of action. Understanding the need to break down your yearly goals quarterly, monthly, weekly and daily will help you reach any goals you set. Set your goals high enough to challenge you, but yet realistic enough to be attainable.

10. You MUST know your MUST - Your MUST is what drives you. For me, my granddaughter Lola is my MUST. She was born with a rare disease called Sturge Weber Syndrome. You can check out her site at www.LolasGift.com. I have always been driven to achieve success and always had small MUSTs along the way, but once Lola was born, everything changed. Since then, each year I realize that in order for us to find better treatments and possibly a cure someday, I need to involve myself more in fundraising. The only way I can do this is by building my company so I can take myself out of my company. This is no easy feat, but whenever I get tired or stressed, I look at her beautiful face and my strength is renewed.

   So what is your MUST? Why do you want to succeed? Do you have children who you would like to give a better life? Or maybe you want to be able to send your children or grandchildren to college. Do you have the dream of retiring at a certain age or being able to devote more time to your passions? I have found that those who have a MUST usually, with the right tools, mentoring and systems, will become successful in whatever they do. For me, I have always wanted to help other people. Through my successes, I have been able to do just that and continue to do so for those researching the cure for and those suffering from Sturge Weber Syndrome. Look at your life and your passion. Build a vision board to help you see your MUST every day. If you don't know what a vision board is, Google it!

   So those are the top 10 reason's Realtors fail. It's probably the last time in this book you will hear me be negative. I could have listed many other reasons, but that could be an entire new book! Please take a moment to reread all these reasons for failure and always keep them in mind. If you find yourself following down the path of negativity, then switch gears and move on. You can be successful in this business. Being a Realtor is probably the easiest thing I have done in my life.

Why did I start this book with how you can fail? The answer is simple: if you understand the challenges ahead of time, you will be able to overcome them with strategy. Today, you begin your Real Estate career. Even if you have been in the business for a while, today you will understand that YOU have the power to make it or break it. What's it gonna be?! Think about it: you get to show homes, meet new people, schedule your life accordingly and make a great living. There are so few businesses you can start for less than $2,000 and earn the huge commissions we earn as Realtors. It's time to Go For It!!!

Chapter Two: A Great Salesperson Never Sells Anything

Helping people while being honest and working hard will always prove successful. Never go for the quick sale. Build a relationship that will last a lifetime and you will have a lifetime of rewards.

My sales career started when I was very young. I was pretty much born with the ability to persuade – it's my best trait. My first "business" was convincing kids in my neighborhood to ride on my dog's back. I charged 10 cents for a ride and had no problem getting many takers. At 6 years old, I realized making money was fun. This business probably lasted a couple of weeks at best, but it was the beginning of it all.

I never received any formal sales training. I did go to a seminar when I was in my early 20s, but I wasn't impressed. I sat through several hours listening to a man trying to sell me his training material, when I realized this was not the salesperson I wanted to be. I knew there must be a better way to sell something and to make people happy about their purchases. This book shares my philosophy for becoming a top salesperson.

Recently, I was flipping through some old papers and found my high school diploma along with a letter that was the catalyst for changing my entire life. The simple letter contained a tool I have taught to hundreds and hundreds of people over the years. It said to use the mirror to analyze yourself.

The truth of the matter is, you can't lie to

yourself if you are looking deep into your own eyes in a mirror. It's easy to rationalize, but as soon as you look into your eyes, the truth comes out. Looking in the mirror – usually my bathroom mirror – has shaped who I am as a salesman and more importantly, who I am as a person. I am always honest because I don't want to face my own wrath when I look at my reflection. If I do anything wrong, believe me, I am going to scold myself!

LESSONS FROM BUSINESS SUCCESSES – AND FAILURES

You have to believe in what you are selling and you must have confidence in your knowledge of what you are selling. You have to believe!

I find selling very easy. I have sold so many things in my life, from corporate paintball programs to flowers in convenience stores. I have sold dating service memberships, lawn care, long distance, Internet programs, marketing ideas and houses. There is only one thing in common with all these sales positions. I have always been #1. I really don't know what it's like to be #2. I have heard about it, but have no desire to be there!

My last and current business is Real Estate. I remember the first day I was hired by my Broker. I told her I would work a minimum of 60 hours a week and would be #1 in her company by the end of my second year. It was a little disturbing when she and an Agent with many years' experience snickered at my comment. They had never seen the power of my sales technique. Now that I have been in this business for a while, I can understand their doubts. Most people don't want to work hard to accomplish their goals. They just coast along being mediocre.

One of my favorite sayings, "Good is the evil of Great," is from the book *Good to Great* by Jim Collins. Most people are happy being mediocre and never accomplish their full potential because they feel they are "good." I always strive to be "great." I have a hard time understanding why some people never strive to become more. They stay in their comfort zone and never work to be the *best* at what they do. Of course, when you find people that work hard to be the best – not just talk about it – those are your best employees or sales reps. These are the people who want to be #1. My Broker is now my partner in my Real Estate company! It just shows how people can change their views.

I'm going to quickly take you through my working career, not to hit on every company or job, but enough so you can understand my work life and the lessons it has taught me.

My first real sales job was selling modular homes. I wasn't sure what I was doing but I knew if I wanted to make money, I would have to sell these homes that were uncommon at the time. I placed an ad in the paper and the appointments started pouring in. Within a week I had sold two homes, which earned me $10,000 in commissions. It was pretty cool.

However, that enterprise was short-lived because I really didn't like the work. The part I really enjoyed was meeting with the couples and pitching the homes. (In hindsight, I should have stuck with Real Estate, since I eventually ended up there.) I think I knew at that point I was destined to be my own boss and always be involved in sales. Of course, if you own your own company, you are always in sales.

That was my first real venture into sales since my six year old self had had his doggy-rifle debut. I had no training and no marketing experience. I just did what made sense and told the truth. I have never lied or extended the truth to make a sale. This is my first and probably most important tip for success: **Never jeopardize your integrity for a buck.** As you will see, I have made good money and lost just a little more, but I always did it honestly.

My next business was probably the most fun. In the early 1980s I started Survival South with one of my best friends. It was a paintball business where as many as 150 people a day would run around 60 acres shooting paintballs at each other while trying to capture the flag. Survival South kept me in great physical shape!

I spent entire weekends playing paintball and spent the rest of the week playing tennis with my partner. This business generated many of the tools I currently use. We were usually sold-out by the end of March for all the weekends in the entire year. Realizing that we had capped our earnings, I came up with the idea of using paintball as a stress-reduction course for corporations during the work week. It was an immediate success.

I didn't realize at the time that I was creating my sales technique. I would walk into major corporations dressed in my camouflage uniform and talk with presidents and CEOs, explaining the benefits of having their sales staff play paintball against their management staff or having management play against laborers. I was too inexperienced to know how difficult this cold calling was. I just walked in and did it. I believed in what I was talking about and I knew how much fun paintball was, and it didn't matter if you were a factory worker or a CEO when you were on the field. Everyone was equal.

The results were amazing. The more corporations I brought on, the more confidence I gained. This is another major lesson: **You have to believe in what you are selling and you must have the confidence in your knowledge of what you are selling. You have to believe!**

Survival South was a success. If it wasn't for personal issues between my partner and me, I would most likely be living in Massachusetts and opening fields around the country. It wasn't meant to be. Instead, I learned a hard lesson about partnerships and trust: I could not lie, while my partner could not tell the truth. We were doomed as a partnership from the beginning. The truth was told when we split the company. Being honest paid off for me. If nothing else, I learned that being honest and having fun are great ingredients to success.

After I sold my paintball business, I bought a business where I placed flowers on consignment in different locations and hoped they sold. The potential for this business was incredible but it wasn't very exciting. I hired someone to deliver the flowers and I bought a restaurant – big mistake!

I knew nothing about the restaurant business and was not used to working 130 hours per week. Within a year I lost everything. The business cost me $1,500 a week, my dad was very sick and I ended up in the hospital. I sold the flower business to keep the restaurant going – another major mistake. Less than two years after selling my paintball business, I was completely broke. I lost my house, my condo, my cars, everything.

Four months later my dad died. The universe works in mysterious ways – I got to spend the last few months of my dad's life with him. I wouldn't change that for anything. I learned more about my dad in that short time than I had learned my entire life.

It was the early 1990s. I had no money, no job and I was devastated over my dad's death. I wasn't sure what I was going to do with the rest of my life. I had two great kids to support. This was the first time in my life I regretted not getting my college degree.

Getting a job was very difficult. I took a job selling MCI long distance when it first came out and it was MCI versus AT&T. I worked with 70 salespeople across different shifts. It was the first time I competed with others for sales. An average shift would consist of 4 or 5 salespeople working at county and state fairs as well as other events. Our job was simple: give away a cooler or another promotional product and get people to switch from AT&T to MCI. I really believed in MCI and their discounted services. Again, you have to believe!

Within a couple of days I was selling a ton of "switches." I would average 60-70 switches per shift (4 hours) compared to everyone else selling 10-15. The company approached me about training other reps in my techniques. However, they didn't want to pay extra for my expertise. A sales manager's job was available, but the person who received it was a friend of the boss. This experience solidified my desire to work for myself. I was never into the games played in the corporate world.

The company continued to pursue me to train other reps but I wasn't going to do it for free. However, I had made a few friends and decided to train them. Within a week their sales shot up to my level. Funny thing, we brought on so much business the company felt it was paying too much in commissions and ended the program. Unfortunately, I was making a good amount of money and really liked what I was doing. The next couple of years were difficult for my family. We scraped by through a series of small business ideas. Some worked and some didn't.

I realized I had a powerful sales presence and a few things remained constant with my sales approach: I was always honest, I tried to help my customers and I always believed in what I was selling. I never did anything to jeopardize my integrity … and it worked!

One of the lessons I learned from MCI was: **When you own your own business, you are not at the mercy of your boss letting you go or the company shutting down**.

To me, selling is very simple. I have read many sales books but when it comes down to results, my techniques work better than anything I have read. First, I believe **a great salesperson never sells anything**.

I'm sure a few of you just said, "What?" The reality is if you truly believe in your product, and you have an honest, sincere desire to help people achieve their goals, then the product will sell itself. **If you help enough people, you will get paid**.

Let's look at one of my other businesses to help understand this concept. My first steady employment after losing the restaurant was working at a dating service. I quickly realized the value of this business for the amount of money it could generate, as well as its benefit for so many single people. Within a short period of time I became the company's sales manager and then the director and vice president. However, what I really want to emphasize is the sales approach.

Dating businesses on the whole have a very high-pressure sales approach. The closing average for this specific national dating service was 46 percent. When I first took over as sales manager, I figured I should sell a few memberships on my own to see what was involved with the sale. I had no training; I just went in and did my thing. As with all my experience in the past, I found it a very easy sell. It was simple – the people were single, we had a way for them to stop being single and it was a classy service. How could they not want to buy a $2,000 membership?

My closing percentage quickly shot up to 87 percent. That was unheard-of in this business. As the manager, my job was to increase sales. So how could I raise the sales average? The answer was quite easy. I had to fire the hard-core, high-pressure sales staff and hire people who really cared about our customers. I hired people with social-service backgrounds and no sales experience that were very caring and loving. Our sales average shot up to 60 percent in no time. So what happened here? **We were honest, sincere, caring and had a true desire to help our customers**. **These are the ingredients to making a sale**.

Sales "experts" will disagree with me and say, "You must have all the sales techniques that have been taught for many years." I don't buy it. You can use this close and that close, and this question and that question, but in the end, people buy because they feel good about what they are buying. Yes, you can make a quick sale here and there, but the lifeblood of a sales career will be lost. You will not receive any referrals.

I want happy customers because they tell their friends to call me. **Referrals are the true measuring stick of how successful you are as a salesperson**.

In short, helping people while being honest and working hard will always prove successful. Never go for the quick sale. Build a relationship that will last a lifetime and you will have a lifetime of rewards.

While much of this book relates to starting a business or to sales, it also relates to everyday life. It is written with 30 years of hard work with virtually no education except what I learned on my own. As you read this book, remember it comes from my heart and soul. It's about how I choose to live my life and how I teach my children, my staff and anyone else who will listen to me.

Chapter Three: Control Your Own Destiny—You Have the Power

No matter how many times you fall, you can always get up again.

There is only one thing in life I fear: lying on my deathbed and saying, "I should have …." That scares the heck out of me. We only have one life and we need to pack as much as we can into that short amount of time. After all, we don't know how much time we have. Some of us will live long lives, while others will die before their time. I watched my mother and father die before they were 60. I watched a best friend's dad die at age 55 after he had been retired for a year. With a little luck I will live a long and fun life. However, I'm not going to spend my life wishing I had done something – I'm going to do it.

I have been an entrepreneur for 30 years now. There were times when I had a lot of money and could buy or do anything I wanted. There were times when I was broke and wasn't sure how I was going to pay my bills. My best asset is my power to **Just Do It**. If I had listened to everyone, I would have finished college and found a job guaranteeing security for me and my family. Sounds like the American dream, doesn't it?

But I knew then what I still know now: **I want to be in control of my own destiny**. The many times I have struggled, I have never failed. Certainly I have lost a lot of money and spent many sleepless nights trying to save a business or two. But I wasn't at the mercy of a company going out of business or having a layoff. I didn't have to deal with office politics. I didn't have a boss telling me what to do, especially when I knew more than he knew. I had the freedom to do whatever I wanted.

The struggles I had were my greatest learning adventures. They taught me and gave me great tools to succeed. They taught me about perseverance and hard work. They taught me about getting back on the horse, because **no matter how many times you fall, you can always get up again**.

Many people have told me they are going to start a business or they have this great idea they want to sell. Business owners tell me they want to grow their businesses and need advice. I would guess maybe 1 percent of the people in the world actually act on their dreams and desires. What a shame. How can you be satisfied with yourself and your life if you haven't tried for what you truly want? How can you look in the mirror when you know you have so much more to offer the world, your family and yourself, and you have done nothing to achieve these dreams? FEAR is the reason you don't go after what you want. "I am too old" or "I don't have enough money" and so on. I'm here today to tell you to: **JUST DO IT!**

To be successful in life you need to take on challenges. You need to look in the mirror and tell yourself you can do anything you want. Have you figured out yet that I like to tell stories? Here is another story of my business life that proves my point.

After working at the dating service for a few years, my desire to be on my own gnawed at me. I knew I wanted to start another business and I really enjoyed the dating business. Not only was I good at generating sales, I really enjoyed offering people insight into their relationships or lack thereof. I helped a ton of people and it felt good. Yup, back to the old "helping people" theme.

I started my own dating service in 1995 when the Internet was just starting to take off. We were one of the first companies to use database integration over the Internet. This meant my members could do all their research from the comfort of their own homes, versus having to come into the office to look at pictures and profiles of other members. Old hat today, but at the time it was an innovative concept.

The funny thing was I didn't know it wasn't something already available, so I searched until I found a software company willing to help me develop what I needed. In the end, I converted my dating service to an Internet-only dating service. However, early on, our office had a break-in where all our computers were stolen. I realized after a year in operation I would have to raise a lot of money to jump-start the business. After all, I was still broke from losing everything only a few years earlier. I put together a small business plan and spreadsheet. The business plan outlined what my company was about, what my goals were and how I was going to reach them. The spreadsheet gave a breakdown of income and expenses over the next 5 years. The potential was excellent.

I had never raised capital before, but I figured as long as I did it honestly and believed in my product, I would be successful. Within days I had money coming in to fund my company. First, I went to family and friends and raised $100,000. I started offering a 1 percent share for $10,000 and by the end of my fundraising, I was selling 1 percent for $100,000. It was amazing. Everywhere I went, people wanted to invest. In three years, I raised more than $3,000,000. The point of this story is if I had listened to the voice whispering how hard this was going to be, I may never had tried. **Just Do It!**

Today is your opportunity. You have an idea or a dream for something you've always wanted to do. **You have the power to make it happen.** For you less-secure risk takers, start your dream part-time. The key is that you start. If you are not sure how to start, just read and learn. Talk to business people who have taken the plunge. We are all willing to tell our stories and to help you create your own story. I have met thousands of small, medium and large business owners and, believe me we love to help others find the "holy grail" of the business life. Learn from them. Buy books. Go online. Research your idea and come up with the best plan you can put into motion. When you come home from your day job, spend another hour or two a day working at your dream. If you work hard, you will be rewarded.

When you finish this chapter, I want you to write down your dream. Then write your long-term goals for how you are going to achieve your dream. Write your short-term goals that will guide you to your long-term goals. You can't do it if you don't try, and if you don't try, you will never forgive yourself. **JUST DO IT!**

Chapter Four: Honesty + Ethics + Desire to Help = SUCCESS

Being honest, sincere, caring and having a true desire to help customers are all the ingredients to making a sale.

Much of what I talk about can be applied to many aspects of life. To me, the most important part of life and how you are judged is through your honesty and ethics. I believe the adage *what comes around, goes around*. I believe in karma. I believe if you live your life as a good person with good intentions you will have a good life. This doesn't mean you won't have your ups and downs, as we all do. It simply means you will bounce back.

Good things happen to good people.

Honesty and ethics are the most important part of my business and personal life. I live every day and guide all my decisions by making sure I am honest and ethical. I would never lie to get a sale. I would never do something that isn't right to make money.

Time for another story:

As I mentioned earlier, one of my first businesses, and definitely one of my favorites, was my paintball business. It was my first partnership, which I believed had many benefits including I got to work with one of my best friends. However, my ex-partner, who I will call Tom, had issues even before we were in business. I should have known better, but I was young and not so smart!

Tom had worked for his mother's business for years, made very good money and pretended to be a good person. There were many times during our friendship I saw him do questionable things. For instance, I remember him telling the electric company he couldn't pay his bill and needed to keep the electricity on because he had a sick child living in his house. Not only did he not have children, he had plenty of money to pay the bill. What was I thinking? I guess I believed I had the power to change him. I saw many good qualities in this guy and thought that with my influence he could become a good person. I was wrong.

During the first few years of our business, he caused us tons of problems, all related to his dishonest dealings with vendors and customers. It always came back and bit him and unfortunately, by association, it bit me too. I remember being on vacation and getting a call from one of our referees. He said the entire staff had quit because Tom treated them terribly, and they would no longer work for him. I took care of our employees and smoothed things over. But I couldn't do that forever.

The final straw came after we had been in business for six years. I had left for my summer vacation and Tom was left to run the business. Each month, one of our money market accounts paid us around $250 in dividends. While I was away, I should have received two checks. When I got back and asked about the checks, Tom said the computers were down and we hadn't received any checks. Of course, I called the company. They had copies of the cashed checks and mailed them to me for verification. Clear as day, my name was scribbled in Tom's handwriting on the back of the checks. I was furious!

Here was one of my best friends whom I trusted, stealing money right in front of me. I ended up going through the books and found many thousands of dollars missing. My first thought was to press charges, but I realized it wouldn't bring the money back and it certainly wouldn't bring back my trust in our friendship. I moved my stuff out of the house we jointly owned and split the company in half. I went my way and he went his. I soon reopened and sold my half, but he never reopened.

Tom lost a business that was making a substantial amount of money; more importantly, he lost his best friend who had been the only person who had put faith in him. What is the moral of this story? I guess it is the old adage again *what comes around, goes around*. Within a week he had lost his business and his best friend. I moved on and continue to be successful in life. To this day I am sure he regrets his actions, although I doubt very much he has changed.

Now, I want you to put yourself in the place of a customer, spouse or friend. Who would you prefer to have a relationship with, an honest person with integrity and ethics, or a person who will tell you what you want to hear whether it is true or not? I try to live my life always asking how I would like to be treated. Most of my business decisions are made with my customers' wishes in mind. After all, **if I don't listen to what they need, I cannot help them and they will not buy**. **It's that simple**.

I need to be inside my customer's heads if I am to help meet their needs. The simple truth is that people want to be involved with honest, hard-working, ethical people. The reason for this is very simple! If you are honest and ethical, your life will change. It is something over which you have complete control. **Honesty + Ethics + Desire to Help = Success**. Of course you have to throw hard work in there too, but success in life comes down to honesty and ethics.

Chapter Five: Getting Started—Just Do It!

If you really desire change, you must make changes. If you really want something, you have to go for it.

People ask me the same question over and over. How do I get started? My simple answer is **Just Do It!** However, this doesn't mean it is *easy* to get started. I have helped many people and each one has different circumstances that determine how they accomplish their goals. Regardless, there are two steps you need to take when you start a business or any venture no matter what your situation.

1.   **Market Research** – If you start this company, you must understand who will be your competition and how they will affect you. How many people need your service? There are many different areas of market research. The key is determining if your business will be able to get past the competition and out to the customer. One of the best ways to do market research is to get a group of people together who potentially may be your customers, i.e., a focus group. Ask them pertinent questions having to do with the product or service you are going to offer. You can learn more from these 1 or 2-hour sessions than you could learn in years of making business mistakes!

2.   **Business Plan** – After you feel confident in your product and or service, then build your plan. **Plans need to be written.** Your business plan can be as simple or as detailed as you like. The plan is a guideline to follow as you start your business. What is your

mission? What are your long-term goals? What are your short-term goals to help you accomplish those long-term goals? What type of marketing will you do? What will your expenses be? If you don't write down everything, these items usually don't happen in an organized way.

Let's look at the person who has enough capital to start the business, but works a full-time job and has a family to support. This person is in a *great* position to start his or her own business. People say they don't have the time to start a business. But if they don't *make* the time, they will never get out of the rat race. **If you really desire change, you must make changes**.

Nothing can change in your life if *you* don't take the steps to make the changes. It's really quite simple. If you are working a full-time job, you are in a prime position to start your own venture. Let's say you are working for a company 8 hours a day. If my math is right, that is only 33 percent of the day. That leaves a lot of time. If you spent an additional 4 hours a day working toward your dream, within a short period of time you will be able to work full-time at it.

It's important to know all about your business prior to starting it. How do you do that? I always recommend working in the industry or for a company that does what you want to do. There is no better way to learn what is involved in running your own venture. If you must, work for free. No business owner will turn away free help! I'm a firm believer in working for free or very little money prior to starting a new company. You will learn things you may want to do. You also will learn things to avoid in your own venture by knowing what NOT to do.

Here are a couple of my own examples of learning while you work. When I started my first long-term enterprise in the 1980s – my paintball business – I was working for a medical lab 60 hours per week. My parents taught me to find a company to work for and stay as long as you could. It was a great job. I worked my tail off, but I was paid very well and was able to buy anything I wanted. When I started Survival South, I did not give up my job. I couldn't afford to have zero cash flow. As with most young people, once I started making money, I got into debt. I bought a new car, some musical recording equipment, etc.

I continued to work 60 hours a week while also working my new company. I did this for a year and a half. At that point, I was generating plenty of money, so leaving my $35,000-per-year job was no problem. I remember walking into my parent's house to tell them I was leaving my job that my mother had gotten for me. My parents were not happy. Of course, they had no idea my company was doing so well. They thought it was just something I did for fun on the weekend. When I told them my new company had $80,000 in the bank after our first year, they supported all my efforts.

This next example is about how I got into the dating industry and eventually the Internet business. I was struggling to make ends meet after losing everything in 1990. It was tough. I started many businesses and looked for a job. I had two little boys to take care of, which was the most important part of my life. I had applied for a job at a dating service, which intrigued me. It was a telemarketing management job for which I had only a little experience. I didn't get hired. I then added telemarketing services to my own marketing company.

After opening telemarketing centers for two companies, I felt I had enough experience to revisit the dating service. I did, and I was hired. After a short time I realized I enjoyed it and wanted to learn all facets of the business. I asked to do sales. I asked to do marketing. I asked to manage the sales staff. I worked with the accountant and learned the business. I did all this extra work without asking for more money. Soon, they asked me to take over and run the company since I had learned all its operations. I was named director and vice president. The entire time I was working, I was planning to someday start my own dating service. From the beginning, when I realized I enjoyed the business and I could make money while helping people, I knew I was going to do it for a living.

For those of you who do not have major obligations, who are just getting out of college or who want to make a change, my advice is to take advantage of your youth and freedom from responsibility. You can conquer the world if you have what it takes – **Just Do It**.

Let's say you just graduated college or high school and you want to start your own business. Obviously you don't have a lick of experience. The next aspect of your education is learning a business. This means getting a job or interning at a company to learn whatever you can in whatever time it takes to accomplish that goal. There is no reason to reinvent the wheel. If you have to work for free during the day, get a night job to have some cash flow. As I have said before, giving away free services will pay you back tenfold. Of course if you can get paid even a small amount of money while learning your new profession, it's a bonus.

While you are learning, it's important you focus on the goal. Learn as much as possible so you can start your own company. However, it's as important to learn what NOT to do as it is to learn what to do. If the company you work for is perfect, then you won't have to make changes. But my guess is that the company is not perfect and there are many changes you will be able to make to improve upon your boss's ideas. **When you see something or learn something, write it down. Write it all down – everything**. Keep all your notes. You will have everything in writing to help formulate your business plan for when you are ready to move on.

Everything I am telling you is simple. **If you really want something, you have to go for it. Just Do It!** Do whatever it takes to accomplish your dreams. There is nothing worse than being on your deathbed thinking you *should* have. You only live once. One of my favorite sayings is, "**Don't let life pass you by, before you live you will probably die**." I wrote that when I was 16 and have tried to live my life with that in mind since.

I believe in Personal Accountability. Over the past many years I have heard every excuse there is for why so many don't accomplish anything in their lives. The funny thing though is it's never their fault. I would like to hear someone say, "I didn't work hard this year and didn't accomplish anything because I was too lazy." Instead I hear on a daily basis things like:

"If I had a better upbringing I would be in better shape."

"My boss treats me terrible so I don't work hard."

"Why should I get a job while I'm getting unemployment?"

"I didn't have enough training."

"My kid had the flu."

"I have been sick all week."

"I was too busy."

"I just don't have the energy for that."

"I'm already working 8 hours a day."

"I don't have any connections."

"I'm afraid of the phone."

"I'm afraid of rejection."

"I don't have any money."

"I'm not good at that."

"The economy is bad."

"I thought about that but I don't think it will work."

"I need to know all the details first."

"If someone would just give me a chance."

I could go on and on with these excuses, as these just come off the top of my head. So why do so many people have so many excuses for why they fail to accomplish their goals? Why do so many people settle for mediocrity? The reason is Personal Accountability. These days, instead of being personally accountable for their actions or lack of actions, it has become acceptable to blame someone else. The problem is that it starts from the top. Look at our politicians. The Republicans blame the Democrats and the Democrats blame the Republicans. Our President tells an outright lie (yes, the "you can keep your insurance" lie) and his follower's say that's okay, he didn't really mean it. If our leadership, whether it is parents, bosses, politicians or community leaders don't accept Personal

Accountability, then who is going to?

The answer is you! You are in complete control of your life and no matter how many excuses you come up with, that won't change. Let's face it, there isn't one person (if anyone is still reading this) that hasn't had a tough time in their life. The difference between those who accomplish and those who blame others for their failures is personal accountability. Personal Accountability. Think about it. What would happen if you looked in the mirror and tried to lie to yourself about why you are not following your dreams? What excuses are you allowing yourself to accept? So many convince themselves of why they are failing instead of what they need to do to be successful. If you are honest with yourself, you will be on your way to accomplishing your dreams!

So I challenge you, yes you. I don't care if you are poor, mentally challenged (I have reading disabilities), tired, uneducated or anything else you use for an excuse. My challenge for you is to throw away all your lame excuses, get off your tail and do what you were meant to do. Stop blaming and start accomplishing. It's not your parent's responsibility, it's not your government's responsibility; it's your responsibility to take care of yourself and your family. It all starts with you and it all starts with Personal Accountability. Go for it!

Chapter Six: The Beginning

Let's understand something right from the beginning. You are starting a business. If you can understand that from the beginning, you will better understand your future. Unfortunately many, if not most, new Agents (and current long term Agents) do not look at their Real Estate business as a business. My job—meaning the management—unlike most other Real Estate companies, is to help you start your business. My job is to educate you, support you and make you be the best Realtor you can become. Is this an easy task? Not at all! Is building a successful business easy to do? Of course not! Can you succeed in this highly competitive business where only 20% of the Realtors account for more than 80% of the business? Follow along as we take you through the systematic steps of becoming successful.

The first step in being successful in any business is to create systems that work. For most Agents starting out, this is a major task. Unfortunately most Agents do not have the business experience to build systems. Others may have the experience but are just not sure how or where to start building systems. My belief is that if you build excellent systems that produce results, then you can become highly successful.

If software alone could sell houses, this would certainly be the best and easiest business in the land. As much as the software is an integral part of internet lead conversion, there is so much more.

Over the next few pages, we will be discussing

all aspects of Realtor sales. Being a Realtor is hard work. Being a successful Realtor is even harder. Let's face it, if everyone could be successful they would. Only the Agents who really want to be successful, the best in their business, are going to succeed. Those are the infamous 20%. You have all heard of them. They are the 20% that stand out from the population. They are the ones that no matter what industry you look at, the best. My goal, my promise to you, is to help you reach that 20%. Do you want to be one of the 20% or one of the 80%? It's not a hard question, but the answer really needs to be thought out. If you accept the fact that you will be working extremely hard and realize that building your Real Estate business is going to take time and effort—a ton of effort—then, you may be able to make it in this business. Yes, **hard work** and **great systems** equals **SUCCESS!**

Chapter Seven: Sales Training

Have you ever wondered why so many people think badly about or look down upon people in the sales industry? It doesn't matter what you sell, you are just a salesman. Why do you think they have those thoughts? The reality is that many salespeople, especially commissioned salespeople, use unscrupulous means of getting consumers to buy things from them. The dishonesty found in the sales industry is horrendous. Some industries work to curb the deceitfulness while others don't. The Real Estate industry tries to keep a handle on it, but unfortunately there are many dishonest and unethical Agents. In a busy market they are scary and in a slow market they are worse. I have trained hundreds, if not thousands, of people in sales during my lifetime. The one ingredient I can't teach is ethics. I personally pride myself on hiring honest and ethical Agents with great personalities. If a person has those qualities, then the sky is the limit.

The one thing that has stayed constant throughout my sales career is the ability to teach people how "not" to sell. Back in the day when everyone was using high pressure tactics to sell everything, I was teaching and using customer service sales. I guess you can call it the Help Sell. Once I got into Real Estate, this method of "not" selling skyrocketed my sales in the beginning and continues to do so year after year. The reality is you don't have to sell anything. There are no real closing techniques. Of course I do teach things that have worked, but nothing that requires any of the deceitful aspects that many sales trainers may teach. There is no "selling" in Real Estate. Maybe more than any industry, Real Estate is the easiest industry to utilize the Help Sell. Best of all you will feel wonderful about "Helping" your customers buy or sell their homes. Not only that, they will think you are great and tell all their friends about how great a Realtor you were and how you helped them find their dream home or sell their current home.

The key to success in Real Estate and any other sales industry is real simple: have fun and help people. That's it. That's the mystery of sales. All those expensive sales training tools currently on the market have one meaning which is to "sell" you how to be a better salesperson. It's salespeople selling salespeople. I love it! It cracks me up. That doesn't mean I believe they are bad people or that their techniques don't work, but most of the seminars I have been to are more "rah rah" sessions than teaching me how to sell something. So go out, have fun, enjoy yourself, help people and most of all smile. You will have a great Real Estate career. The reality is, if every salesperson just followed those four steps, they would most likely double their sales no matter what they sell.

With that said, there are certain things you must do when in sales:

a. Listen – If you learn nothing from the many chapters in this book, this is probably the most important. How many times have you worked with a salesperson and you said to yourself, "I wish he/she would just listen to what I'm saying"? How many sales do you know that salespeople have lost from you because they are not helping you to accomplish your goal? I always like to look at all situations thinking how I would like to be treated. Whenever you doubt anything, just ask yourself if you would like to be treated in that manner. It makes understanding the customer's point of view real easy!

Listening is the most crucial trait you must have or learn to be successful. If you are like me, a little hyper or high strung, then this is something you really need to work on. It took me a long time to learn to stop talking and listen to my customers' needs. Is it tough for an A type personality to listen? Yes, it is! However, once you master this, you have probably mastered the hardest portion of this job.

There are three instances in which you will really need to be sure you are listening. The first is email. Be sure to read and understand everything your customer needs. When you email them responses, be sure to answer everything. I prefer to do this by using what they wrote. For instance, if someone writes me a list of questions, I will type in bold italics the answer to each question below their original question. By doing this you are sure to cover all the bases and not leave any questions unanswered.

The second is on the phone. Be sure to pay attention to details while talking to customers on the phone. It is very important to write down any items that are discussed so they may be addressed. There is nothing worse than your customer asking for something and having to call them back to find out again what they needed. How embarrassing! What do you think they think? What would you think? Listen!

Finally, the next example of important times to

listen, which is just as important as the other two instances, is while showing property. No matter how in depth you discuss their Real Estate needs, things seem to change when you show property. All of a sudden, little things are being mentioned that the Buyers like or dislike about certain properties. It is critical that you listen to their conversation, comments and any questions they may ask. The more you can learn about their needs, the better service you can provide them. It's very important that you utilize the info you receive to go into the next step of sales.

b. Refine – One major mistake I see all the time in Real Estate, which is a result of listening or not listening, is failure to utilize the information that was learned during the listening phase of the Realtor/Customer relationship. Because of this, Realtors are constantly showing 10+ homes at a time. If they had listened properly they would have discovered that 5 of the 10 homes were not what the customers were looking for in the first place. The Realtor could have saved both the customer and him or herself a lot of time. Also, the more homes you show, the more confusing it becomes for your customer. Remember, your job is to help them find their dream home. You need to listen to their needs and then refine their search to best utilize your time together. There are many Agents that will show up to 50 homes before finding the customer a home. Just think how difficult it would be for you to make a decision after looking at 50 homes.

c. Help your Customer – This may sound easy, but it can be very trying and tough some times. I have seen so many salespeople take their customers for granted. In the end, the salespeople with the best results also offer the best customer service. Again, think back to your own experiences. How did you want that salesperson to treat you? Did they listen to what you needed? Did they go out of their way to do more than what was to be expected? Do you? Use your best and your worst experiences in your life to learn how to give the best customer service. Learn from the good, but learn more from the bad. You don't want to end up being *that* person.

A large part of understanding how to give the best customer service is to understand patience. I have seen and heard so many Agents complain about the amount of time they spent with someone. Keep in mind, you can be that salesperson that really only cares about how much time and effort a transaction takes, or you can be the salesperson who does what is best for their customer. Take your time, help your customer and you will receive the best gift of all...referrals!

Okay. So how do you become more patient? Firstly, you need to realize that most people are very nervous about buying their home and many of them are very scared. There is a huge fear in buying a home and by understanding your customer's fear, you will become more patient and more willing to help them. In a short time, their fear will turn to confidence; confidence in you as their Agent. They believe that you will take them on the awesome ride of home ownership. You can be their hero, or you can be their heel. If you are patient while caring about your customer, you will go far!

Let's do a little exercise. Let's break down the amount of time you actually spend with a buyer.

- First contact (telephone) and searches – ½ hour
- 1st Showings – 2 hours
- 2nd Showings – 2 hours
- 3rd Showings – 2 hours
- Writing and submitting offer – 1 hour
- Contract negotiations – 1 hour
- Home inspections – 2 hours (for those of you who go)
- Phone calls to customer – 1 hour
- Phone calls to other realtor – 1 hour
- Misc. – 1 hour

Total time – 13.5 hours. Average Commissions on a $200k house: $3,000 Hourly Rate: $222/hr

Now look at the total actual amount of time you put into that customer and realize that you make a heck of a lot of money for not many hours. This exercise is a great way to understand that we are in an awesome field that requires not a lot of actual time per customer. Why are successful Realtors always working? This is because they are working with many customers at the same time. You must always keep your pipeline full if you plan on being successful in this business. With that said, we have seen many Agents get a few sales in a month and then decide to take time off for the next month. Then they wonder why two months later they have no sales and contracts. If you feel you need to take a little time off, take a week or so, not a month!

Always be patient, understand the fear, always help your customer and always offer excellent customer service. You will succeed in Real Estate.

d. Accurate Answers – One of the reasons many salespeople are successful is the ability to think on their feet. This is both a blessing and a curse. The key to success in sales is product knowledge. In the Real Estate industry it's difficult to really know everything. There are so many variables that affect a transaction. By providing accurate answers, you will usually maintain a smooth transaction. How do you provide accurate answers? What do you say if you don't know the answer? It's easy. Just let them know that you don't know the answer and that you will find it out for them. It doesn't get much easier than that! I have always been a believer of being the source for the source. Keep in mind that everything you tell them creates liability for you. If you don't know the answer and try to give an answer that isn't correct, you are facing problems down the road. It's much easier to get the phone number or website for them to see the answer with their own eyes.

It also limits your liability. Never answer a question in which you don't know the answer. Of course, when you tell them you will find out the answer, do this in the quickest time possible. Remember that they are only working with you, even though you are working with multiple customers. They want their answers yesterday and if you don't provide the answers, they will move on to the next Agent.

Chapter Eight: Educating Customers

One of the most ignored, overlooked, and extremely important aspects of sales is the education of a customer. Your customers are a sponge wanting to learn as much as possible about the entire home buying experience. It's up to you to take them by the hand and walk them through the transaction. Many of your customers may have never bought a house or might have bought a home many years ago. The rules have changed. They may as well be a first time homebuyer.

There are a few areas that you will need to address with your customer right from the beginning of your relationship. By covering these items, you will secure more customers while losing less. After all, the worst thing you can hear as an Agent is, "Thanks for all your help! I bought a house last week!" The worst part is they are all excited and you have to pretend that you are happy for them while thinking that you worked for 6 months with those people and they did this to you! It's the worst!

1.   **Loyalty** – One of the first things I tell my customers is this, "I will give you 150% of my effort to help you find a home. However, by doing that, the only thing I require of you is to be loyal to me."

2.   **New Construction** – This is huge for you. My first advice is to talk to your customer about buying new construction. Offer to take them to all the models in the area and register them with the builders. We have all worked with that buyer who had bought a house through a builder, a builder that has no problem paying

Real Estate commissions. Again you lose. Explain to your customer that one of the reasons consumers use Realtors for buying new construction is to have another set of eyes. We do hundreds of transactions each year and know what needs to be accomplished in new home construction. Remember, we represent them and their interests as Single Agents.

3.   **FSBOs** – Yes, you already know about this one. For Sale By Owner (FSBO) homes are everywhere and if you don't get to them first, your customer might. Educate your customer about how they should call you with the address and phone number of any FSBO they would like to see. It's up to you to talk to the FSBO and ask them if you can bring by your customer, as well as having them sign a commission agreement. The best means of doing this is finding all the available FSBOs in the area in which you are going to be showing your customer properties. You may want to contact them to see if they will work with a Realtor if you brought a customer by. Doing this will help your customer understand that you work with FSBOs too.

4.   **Calling the Listing Agent and Open Houses** – If there is one single thing that burns Agents most it's losing a sale to the Listing Agent. Very few Listing Agents will let you know that your customer is viewing their listing with them and writing a contract. One of the flaws in this industry that is unfortunately very prevalent is the fact that commission salespeople will do whatever it takes to get sales. However, with that said, there are a few excellent Agents, like our Agents, that will always do the right thing. It may hurt sometimes, but you will always be able to look in the mirror and know the truth! Be sure to educate your

customer that if they see a home they would like to view, they call you so you can make the necessary arrangements.

The more you educate your customer the better. It is okay they know that you only get paid if they buy a home from you. Let them know you appreciate them as a customer which is why you will give them 150% effort. More importantly, prove it. We have had many customers not buy a home because the FSBO wouldn't pay our Agent. Your customers will become loyal to you as long as you do what you say and are extremely dedicated to their home search.

Chapter Nine: Follow-Up

When I first started in Real Estate my Broker said three things that stuck with me…Follow up, Follow up, Follow up. It is so important and simple, but is also very overlooked. What happens when you show someone a few homes and they don't buy right then? Usually they go back to where they came from and you move on to the next customer who needs your immediate help. In many cases, you will lose that customer. While you are out helping your newest customer your old customer is still doing their homework and still want to buy a home. It's great that you have them in the 100MPH Marketing system, but that is not enough. All customers need to be serviced. The customers that have actually been with you to view homes will almost always buy a home in the future. If you are strong enough to continue to follow up and help these customers, you will be their Agent.

A good CRM software program will help you in your customer follow up. However, nothing will replace the need for phone calls to your customers. It's important to have a call back system that will put you in front of your customer not only by email, but by voice. We have found that even if your customer is receiving listing updates, they are still online doing their own research. For this reason, it is imperative that you follow up with phone calls.

Let's look at a scenario. You are the buyer. You go onto your website and do a search. The next thing you know you have received three emails within the first few hours. By the end of the day you have received a phone call from the Agent to discuss your needs.

Great customer service with a great response rate! You are informed by your Agent that you will be receiving updates on a regular basis of all the new listings. You are excited to have someone on your side while you are looking for a home…even if you won't be buying for 6 months.

A month goes by and you are still receiving your updates of new listings. In fact, over the month you have subscribed to a few different sites and are receiving listings from a few Agents. Of course since you are serious about finding a home, you never stopped looking online at new houses. Fast forward 6 months. You are not sure who the first Agent was that helped you, but that's okay because you have three Agents sending you listings. Fortunately, one of the Agents stayed in touch by phone. That Agent is the Agent you call to set up your showings. You go out and buy a home. Once you have purchased, you send a letter to the other Agents stating, "Thank you so much for your help in buying my home. You can take me off your list now as I bought a home last month. Thanks again! Oh, if you are ever in the area, don't hesitate to stop by and see my beautiful new home."

As you can see by that scenario, the Agent who stayed in touch won! They always will. If you put yourself in the customer's shoes, you will understand this much better. As we all know, there is nothing worse than getting the above scripted email. Remember, Follow up, Follow up, Follow up!

Now you know how to be an effective, efficient and productive sales person. Always remember not to "sell" anyone. Always help them. Educate your customers. Listen to your customers. Handle your customers with respect and patience. Follow up with your customers. Finally, look into your eyes in a mirror every day and ask yourself, "Am I doing the best I can do at everything?" When you can finally say, "Yes," to that question, you have succeeded.

Chapter Ten: The Sales Process-- Showings

As you continue your phone calls and emails, your appointments will start to become a reality. You are now on the path to becoming busy, probably busier than you will be prepared for over the next several months.

1. Once you have a customer who emails or calls you letting you know when they are coming, it is imperative that you talk to this person by phone. I have seen many Agents lose customers simply because they didn't call the customer prior to their arrival to our county. On this phone call it is time to address the properties they want to see as well as the details of their visit.

2. Once you have your appointment and the details of their needs, it is time to do a search for the most current homes available to your customer. If you listened to their needs, you should be able to limit the number of homes to be shown out of the multitudes of homes available.

3. After you have determined the best properties, print out the full Agent version of each listing. In a situation where you have more than 10 homes to show, you will need to narrow the search. I have always done this by picking the best homes. I know that might sound ridiculous, but I have seen many Agents show 12-15

properties in a day for multiple days in a row. The customer doesn't buy a home, most likely because they have seen to many homes and are very confused. If you do a great job of listening, you may show them 10 homes the first day and less each consecutive day you show. If you are an excellent listener, this is pretty easy. If you are like many of us ADD salespeople (like me) it may be very difficult. Unfortunately, if you don't become an excellent listener, you will have trouble succeeding in the Real Estate world.

4. Schedule appointments to view properties. Give yourself an hour spread at each property you plan to show. For instance, if you are going to show a property at 11am, schedule the showing time between 10:45 and 11:45. This allows for being early or late. Most showings take approximately 15 minutes. It is important to map out the best possible route in which to show property. We find that the Streets Software from Microsoft works great. Of course these days you can also use a personal GPS to get from property to property.

5. If at all possible, **show the best house on the list 2nd to last**. This is about the only "sales" thing that I do. The reason for this is simple. If they look at houses all day, but are not completely impressed, then they look at a house that fits exactly what they are looking for, they are more likely to act. The final house will confirm that the 2nd to last house is by far the best.

6. Do not "Sell" anyone. Sometimes the less said the better. It is okay to make comments; however, never make a negative comment about a property. Your tastes and their tastes may be completely different. They might feel that they have found a diamond in the rough and your negativity causes them to wonder if you know what you're doing, or worse, if you are the right Agent to help them find their new home.

7. Always write the offer. Never talk your customers out of writing an offer, even if the offer is very low. Firstly, we are required by our Real Estate rules to write any offer that a customer would like to present. I have actually seen Agents talk their customers out of writing offers and telling them to go home and think about it. This may be applicable sometimes, but when a customer wants to write an offer, write it!

8. Before you can write the offer, you need to make sure that the offer price is not too high and not too low. We do this by pulling up comparable properties, located in the same neighborhood or close neighborhoods. I prefer to come up with the average price and adjust that amount depending upon the condition of the homes. We will go over that shortly while doing CMAs.

9. There are many different situations you may find yourself in when writing an offer. You will understand this as we move on through the different options available. Your Broker or Team Leader will always be there to help

negotiate and go through all your dealings. Most offers are straightforward. You simply fill in the blanks of the contract using Zip Forms or Forms Simplicity (or whatever your Broker wants you to use). However, many customers want the seller to pay a portion of closing costs. Keep in mind that the seller is only allowed to pay up to 3% of customers closing costs and prepaids. (Occasionally a lender will allow up to 6 %.) There are other forms not on Zip Forms that must be filled out. These include the Home Inspection Rider, Home Owners Association Disclosure, Mold Disclosure, etc.

10. Once the offer is written, you must go over the entire contract with the customer. It is imperative that everything is filled out, read and signed by your customer. They must understand what they are signing. It is very important that you learn every portion of the contract and understand it first, because ultimately you will have to go over the contract in detail with your customers.

11. Once your customer understands the contract and signs it, you need to be sure to get the escrow check. It is important that you let them know the check will be deposited. This check must be given to the office manager within 24 hours. Now you need to make copies of everything for your buyer. Make sure you give them a copy of their check, contracts and Association Docs.

12. Now that you have an executed offer, you need to submit this offer to the Seller's Agent.

Simply call them and let them know you have an offer. If they are a local company, it is always better to bring the offer to the Agent in person. If not, fax it to them.

Chapter Eleven: The Offer

Here's how this works:

a.   Submit the offer

b.   Explain the counteroffer to your buyer

c.   Submit another counteroffer

d.   Final Agreement and signatures

The offer is the most important part of your sales process. First of all, if you get an offer, you might get a contract. If you have a contract, you might get to closing. If you get to closing…..you get paid! What a concept!

Before you write the contract, you want to see if the home is priced correctly. To do this, simply search the MLS for sold, active, contingent and pending properties within the past 6 months. I then figure out the average square foot price. Just take the cost of the home and divide it by total sq. ft. For example, a $200,000 priced home divided by 2000 total sq. ft. = $100 per square ft.

After I do several of these (preferably 6), I get the total price per sq. ft and take an average. Now take the square footage of the listing and multiply it by the average price per sq. ft. This should get you close to your sales price. After you have finished writing your contract, it is time to submit it. Most Realtors these days are faxing contracts. It is always better to make a copy and drop the contract off in person. Either way, call the Realtor and let him or her know that you are in the process of sending over an offer. I usually give them 24 hours to answer the offer.

Now you sit and wait. You will receive your counteroffer usually in a timely manner. Now it is up to you to meet with your Buyers and go over the counteroffer. Most of the time they will limit the D & N (repair clauses). You need to sit with your buyer and show them the numbers you have come up with to justify the counteroffer. If you are having trouble accomplishing this, you can call the other Realtor and ask them to justify the price. 99% of the time you can do this without asking them. I have on a few occasions asked them to produce comps to justify their price. Keep in mind that once you receive a counteroffer the original offer is null and void.

Once you have determined the price that your Buyers are either willing to accept or would like to use as a counteroffer, you simply call the other Agent and let them know you are sending over the signed counteroffer. All offers and counteroffers should have signatures. Occasionally, we will do this over the phone if it is difficult to get together with your Buyers or their Sellers. However, it is not a contract until everyone signs everything.

Once you have all come to an agreement you want to get signatures immediately. You must have these as soon as possible. Deals are lost many times when Realtors decide to get the signatures tomorrow. Almost guaranteed, a better offer will come in before the morning, and Selling Realtor is obligated to present this new offer to the seller.

Now that you have gone through the entire negotiating process, you need to pat yourself on the back. But don't congratulate yourself for too long. It's time to start the closing process, which involves ordering inspections, ordering surveys, and talking to lenders. Let the fun begin!!!!

Chapter Twelve: Floor Time

Fact: The average amount of floor calls nationwide that are converted into customers are 2%.

When I first started in the business, I was told not to waste my time on floor calls. Nobody ever bought anything because they were just looking. I didn't buy it! I believe that you have a purpose to a phone call; to convert the call to a customer. The key is being prepared and understanding how to handle the phone calls. My first year I had 36 sales, 28 of them were floor calls. So much for the myth that floor calls are a waste of time. Most of my Agents have been able to convert floor calls fairly easily. Follow our floor call system and you too will be converting calls in no time!

Firstly, you need to be prepared for floor. On a daily basis, your in-house inventory will be changing. Some homes will go under contract, some homes may expire, some homes might be withdrawn or a myriad of other possibilities. If you do not review the floor book each time you are on floor, how can you expect to convert the phone call to a customer?

There are two aspects to our floor time: MLS and Live Chat (not all Brokers have live chat).

Both of these programs should be open at all time while you are on floor. You must be prepared for a phone call at any times during your shift. It is not advisable to be making phone calls to your customers while on floor. If a floor call comes in and you are not available, it will go to another Agent in the office. Our customers always come first. I think you understand that by now.

Chapter Thirteen: Using the MLS to Capture a Lead

Your personality will be the first contact with your new potential customer. Many times a person calls just to get a price of a home. Already assuming you are going to try to sell them something, they are very tentative and their guard is up! As I have said many times, if you can have fun, you can win. I usually answer the phone with something to catch the caller off guard. A simple, "Good Morning" when it is the afternoon will always get a chuckle, or "Are you having a fun day?" at any time will do the same. It's tough sometimes, but if you can't break the ice you will have difficulty converting the call to a customer.

Let's go through a typical phone call. This will illustrate how a good floor call should go.

Agent – Tropical Realty, this is Mitch, how can I help you? Are you having a fun day today?

Customer – I guess it's a fun day! By the way it's afternoon not morning.

Agent – Oh yeah, time just flies while I'm having fun here! So what can I do for you?

Customer – I would like to know the price for (insert street address)

Agent – Great let me pull that up and I can take a look. This will only take a minute. So are you local or out of state?

Customer – I'm in Boston.

Agent – I'm from Boston too (if you are lucky

enough to make that bond, you are all set. You should be able to get them easily as a customer). I've been down here about 9 years and I love it. It's the best thing I ever did. Are you currently working with a Realtor?

Customer – No, I'm just starting to look and I found your website online.

Agent – That's how most people find us. Most of our customers come from the North. Are you looking for a vacation home or are you moving down here permanently?

Customer – I'm thinking about moving down there for good. I'm sick of the cold!

Agent – I understand that one! What type of home are you looking to buy?

Customer – I'm looking in Cocoa Beach. I've always wanted to live near the Ocean. I need at least 3 bedrooms and 2 baths.

Agent – How big a home do you want?

Customer – At least 1800 sq. ft.

Agent – Okay, I got the info on the home you called on. It's $285k. When are you going to be coming down here to look at houses?

Customer – Next Month.

Agent – Do you have to sell you home first?

Customer – No, I currently rent and it's time to buy. I'm tired of throwing money away.

Agent – It's true, for what you pay for rent up there I can help you find a home to buy. Well, while we were talking I pulled up a list of properties including the listing you called on. There are 25 others that are similar. Would you like me to send you the list so you can look at them?

Customer – I don't want to waste your time in case I don't come down there.

Agent – Not a problem. I'll also set you up in our listing update system, which will notify you of any new listings that come on the market. What's your email address and I'll send you the list.

Customer – Billy@BillyBoy.com

Agent – Great! I'll send it right up to you. Could I have your name and phone number. I would like to check in with you to see if you have any questions or would like me to change the homes I'm sending.

Customer – Sure, my name is…..

Agent – Great, I'll give you a call in a few days to go over the listings and I can start to put together a list of properties to show you next month when you come down.

You have now created a lead, a very strong lead. Many times the customer will be local, but they may also be from anywhere in the world. Many times they are looking at your website, and the property they are calling on is located in your IDX system. If it is not on your list of in-house listings, you need ask if they have the MLS number. They usually do. The few key points you need to take from this dialogue are:

a. "Are you working with a Realtor?" – I'm not a big fan of doing other Realtor's work. Ethically we are not allowed to try to steal the customer if they call on one of our listings. You will find over time that most Agents will try to steal your customers. It's the nature of this beast. However, all of our Agents are required to be the best and most ethical and honest

Agents in the county. We don't lower our standards because they lower their standards.

    b. Find something in common quickly – If you can create a common bond quickly, you can almost guarantee winning this person over. I use golf because it relates to leisurely sunny days while relaxing. Everyone can relate to the sun and relaxation.

    c. Send them a list – Be sure to get their email address to send them a list. Once you have them set up in your prospecting system, you will be in front of them on a regular basis.

    d. Get their phone number – Of course the ultimate goal is to get their phone number so you can follow up, eventually get the appointment and show houses when they come down.

    e. Get the appointment – If they are a local lead, your goal is to set an appointment. A simple "would you like to see any of these?" works. You can't get what you don't ask for. Ask for the appointment and you will be pleasantly surprised!

Chapter Fourteen: Live Chat

Many websites have a live chat button. With this, a customer visiting your site has the opportunity to instant message you. The system works just like any other Instant Message (IM) system you might have used in the past. Simply handle the IM like you would handle a phone call. Hopefully you can type quick enough to keep up with your potential customer.

When Live Chat is open, a customer has the ability to IM you. Once they initiate the contact, you will need to react quickly. If you don't react quickly enough they will be gone. From the point of contact until the end of the IM, you will follow the same scenario as a floor call. There is no difference, with the exception that it's all type versus voice. Once you have finished the conversation, you will print the conversation and continue the process.

Chapter Fifteen: 11 Things to Get You Started in Real Estate

So now you have gone through your training and are ready to go. But where do you go from here? How do I actually get business?

1. First, you need to put together a list of every person you know. You should include friends, acquaintances, relatives, coworkers and anyone else. The more names you can compile, the better your chance of success.

2. Schedule an open house for every weekend. If you are not going to be showing property, spend at least 2 hours on a Saturday or Sunday at an open house. This is a great way to acquire local Buyers with the possibility of finding a buyer for the home you are keeping open.

3. Start Farming an area. Post cards are a proven success in the Real Estate world. Of course there are many Agents that currently farm certain areas. Fortunately for you, most Realtors don't do a great job of this.

4. Volunteer. The more you do for your community, the more the community will do for you. Get out and help your fellow neighbor. It could be just a few hours per week, but the return will be plentiful. Not only is it good for business, it is good for the soul!

5. FSBOs. Stop by a For Sale By Owner and ask them if they would like help in selling their property. The biggest mistake most Realtors make is to

try to get the listing. My approach is to let them know you are there to help them once they find a buyer. You will supply them with a Sellers Disclosure, a Contract and other disclosures as needed. Let them know that if they need help writing the contract, you will gladly help at no charge. The reality is that 90% of all FSBOs turn to Realtors. They will remember the Realtor who tried to help them not sell them!

6.   Internet Marketing. Internet marketing is great as long as you have a system in place to capture leads as well as convert them. The average conversion rate for Internet leads is less than 1% nationally. The reason most Agents fail with Internet Leads is their lack of systems in the areas of their email marketing and phone call follow up on a consistent basis.

7.   Expired Listings. This is a little trickier and work intensive to do but many Realtors have been successful with approaching people whose listings have expired. Usually the listing was overpriced and that is why it didn't sell. You must check the MLS to see the properties that have expired each day. At that point you need to research and get the Seller's phone number. Keep in mind that there are probably other Realtors trying to get the listing. You must be timely in contacting them to get your name in front of them first.

8.   Join a health club, yoga club or some other form of fitness. You may ask why? Not only is it good and healthy for you to join a club, but it also puts you in a situation where you are meeting lots of people. I'm a big believer in networking as much as possible. People like to do business with people that have similar interests. For the same reason I also believe that joining different groups or sports teams such as softball, golf,

baseball, hiking, activity groups and so on will all help you build your business.

    9.   Seminars. Sharing your knowledge with the community is a great way to show you are an expert. Whether it is investments, first time Homebuyers, schoolteacher, other community programs (nurses, police, firefighters), or 1031 exchange programs, the more you appear to know, the more you will gain!

    10. Education. You can never learn enough. Enroll in as many classes as possible. Designations are not overly important in your success although many will argue that belief; however, if you take just one thing away from each class, you will be a more successful Realtor.

    11. Work Full Time. This is a full time business. The biggest percentage of successful Realtors work between 40-60 hours per week. If you are not working at least this much, chances are you won't succeed in this business. Many Agents have the tendency of making a few dollars and then slowing down the momentum they worked so hard to obtain. You need to always take the time to prospect and keep the pipeline full. No matter how busy you are currently, it won't take long for the well to dry!

Chapter Sixteen: Circle of Influence

Your first step in being successful is letting everyone know you are a Realtor. Start compiling a list immediately of everyone you know. Be sure to include their name, address, phone number and email address. You should be entering this information into some form of database for easy merging with letters. You can find this program in the newer versions of Microsoft Office.

In compiling your list you need to think of your relatives, neighbors, friends and anyone else you might have even a casual relationship with, such as teachers, members of your church or temple, etc. Also, be sure to include relatives and friends from out of state. Remember, if you are in a retirement or second home/vacation area, I can guarantee one of your friends or relatives know someone who is moving in your area. They can be a great source of referrals. The more names you can compile, the more people will know you are a Realtor.

Once you have completed your list, the next step is to write a letter. I prefer letters versus post cards for this mailing. The letter should be similar to the letter below:

Dear (friend),

I just wanted to take a moment and let you know that I have switched careers and am now a Full Time active Realtor. I have decided to work for (Brokerage) as from my research; they are one of the most ethical and honest companies around. At (Brokerage) everyone works as a team, which is great for new Realtors. We are never alone in dealing with Real Estate transactions. They help every step of the way!

My goal as a Realtor is to help you with all your Real Estate needs. If you or someone you know is looking to buy, sell or rent a home or condo, please take a moment and call me. I am committed to my new profession and will work hard to help anyone.

I look forward to hearing from you!

Of course your letter may be any variation of this letter. Be sure to put it on nice stationary and use nice envelopes. Remember that in this business you need to be as classy as possible without being unapproachable.

With a week or so from mailing the letter, you should call everyone to be sure they received it, and to see if they know anyone buying or selling. After your first mailing, you will then keep in touch with them through the email program you have chosen. This is a very affordable way to stay in front of the people who are closest to you. The key to this is to be in front of them when they think about Real Estate. You can help sell a home anywhere in the world. It's important that your circle of influence knows you are there to help them even if you don't live anywhere near them. Referral fees are a great source of income. In my last year of selling homes, prior to opening my brokerage, I earned an extra $20,000 in referrals alone.

Chapter Seventeen: Open Houses

Open houses are a great source for generating buyer and seller leads. You might only get a couple of people who stop by, but if you are fun and enjoyable to talk to, there is a good chance they will turn into customers. Most people that go to open houses are not represented by a Realtor. This is your opportunity.

Open houses take a certain type of mindset. You will hear from many Agents that they are a waste of time. During my first two years in the business, all my listings came from open houses.

I believe you should work an open house. This means the hours from 10am – 4pm. Most Realtors only work from 1pm – 3pm. You don't even have enough time to have people stop by. As I mentioned earlier, if you are going to build your business, you need to act like a business.

If you are going to commit to doing open houses, then you should be doing them every week at the same house until it sells. You want the other listings in the neighborhood to see your commitment to selling that house.

Let's discuss picking the right house. You should pick a home that has an average house price in the area. For instance, the average sale price in my area is $250,000. Most sales are between $200k and $350k. The house I want to work an open house at would be in the $250k - $300k price range. This is the most common priced sale.

Next, I want to pick a neighborhood that has at least 3-5 more listings in the neighborhood. I want them to see me there every weekend. We know that most Realtors don't do a great job of following up with their customers or keep their flyer box full. When consumers who have their home listed with someone else see you there, they will come to talk to you at some point. Consistency is the most important aspect of any marketing program.

Setting up the open house is critical to your success at generating visitors. You should have as many directional signs as you can. The more signs pointing people toward your open house the better. Most Realtors just put a sign out front and hope that people come. We recommend having balloons on your directional signs as well as on the mailbox in front of the house. The more fun and inviting it looks, the more people will stop by!

Inside the home there are a few things to keep in mind. Open as many shades and blinds as possible. Let the sunshine in! With the owner's permission, bake some cookies, light some candles, have refreshments and have fun.

Keep in mind that potential customers may be interviewing you for a listing. Many times people searching for a Realtor to market their home will go to open houses to find a Realtor. It is important to always smile and be professional. The more fun you have the greater your chance of being successful.

Let's look at the numbers. If you do an open house 4 times per month you will average a minimum of 8 different Buyers and or Sellers that come through the door. Based on an average Realtor's closing rate, you should get at least 1- 2 sales per month.

One of the first questions most Realtors will ask is, "Are you working with a Realtor?" You should ask this question, but it needs to be asked in a different manner. Ask it like this: "Which Realtor in town are you working with?" The reason we ask it like this is that they are less likely to say they are working with a Realtor if they aren't working with a Realtor. Asked the other way, they can simply say yes (even though they don't have a Realtor) and you have hurt your chances of becoming their Realtor.

Chapter Eighteen: Farming

Everyone talks about farming an area, but surprisingly not many Realtors actually do Farming. What is Farming? Farming is developing a marketing program to a specific neighborhood or area and continuing to do most of your marketing in that area. I'm a big believer in picking the area you live. Many people in the neighborhood might already know you and who better to sell their home than a qualified Realtor who resides in the same area. You should be Farming to a minimum of 500 homes if not 1000 homes. Statistically speaking, if you market to 1,000 homes you should receive 50 sales per year from the farmed area.

Before you can start Farming, you need to become an expert in that area. You should know which schools serve the neighborhood, local businesses, amenities, area of interests and activities. You need to know everything! The more you know, the more you will be asked for answers. The more answers you give, the more business you will receive.

You will become an expert in your area. Now, the fun begins. There are many means of marketing an area. We will touch on a few of them.

1. **Post Cards** – Post Cards have been my marketing tool of choice over the years. Unfortunately, most Realtors don't have a plan when they do post card marketing. They simply send out a post card once every month or so and wait. Although they may receive a sale or two from this, it is not the correct procedure to utilize

direct mail. Proven Direct Mail works the following way. Send out one post card per week for 8 weeks to the same households. You should do at least 500 homes but it is more effective if you send direct mail to 1000 or more homes. After the first introduction mailing, include different coupons for a local businesses on each post card. Once the initial 8 weeks are done, continue to mail twice monthly. Repetitive direct mail works best.

    2.   **Neighborhood Parties** - This is another great way to meet your neighbors as well as generate business. I think that family parties are a great idea. Have a neighborhood cookout, ice cream social, swimming party. Camp out in your backyard or barbecue on game day. Other parties could include woman's night out, golf party, book clubs and Sunday football parties.

    3.   **Neighborhood Seminars** - Informational seminars will usually generate a lot of interest. Some of these could include Financial planning, Buying or Selling Investment Real Estate, Selling your home tips, Travel Ideas, etc. The more creative the better.

    4.   **Neighborhood Improvements** – Send a letter to your farm area and let them know you are interested in making the neighborhood a more beautiful place to live. Form a neighborhood committee to take on projects such as beautifying median strips and entrances, helping a neighbor that might be in need or planting flowers in common areas.

    The key to all of this is to get involved with the neighborhood in which you want to do business. The more involved you are in helping the area become a better place to live, the greater your chances of being successful. People realize and respect those that help.

Help and you will receive.

Chapter Nineteen: Join a Club

The hardest part of getting started is to put yourself in a position to meet as many people in your community as possible. The more people you meet, the more people that will know you are a Realtor, and the more chances of them using you as a Realtor. In the beginning of your career, you especially need to get your name and face out there.

You should always have your car signs on your car and your name badge on your clothes when going to these places. What types of places should you go to? Join a club or club that you are interested in being a participant. It doesn't make sense to join a club that has to do with art if you have no desire to learn about art. You can join a health club (one of my favorite), an athletic group, a book club, an art club, an activity club, a boating club, a music club, a leads group, a bowling league or any of the other great groups and clubs that are out there. There are some clubs for people from different areas. In my town, there are organizations for those from Boston and New York, or who share common backgrounds, like Italian or Cuban-American clubs. Those are great places to meet people who you already have something in common with. Be the life of the party, and they will all know who you are and what you do. People like to work with people that have similar interests.

When I first got in this business I joined multiple clubs. I wanted to learn how to golf so I volunteered at a golf course as a ranger. I drove around handing out business cards and meeting people. I also got to play golf for free and golfed almost every day for two years! One of my passions in life is baseball. It's a sport I played since I was 6 until I was 46. I also joined a bowling league and a Ping Pong league. I was always *business* and sold many homes through each of these clubs. You can never get enough exposure so why not have fun while you are drumming up business!

Chapter Twenty: Volunteer

I know I talk about community a lot, but to me this is where you live. You need to give back to the community if you expect the community to give to you. There is no formula to volunteering, no advice I can give you, and this is not required by any means. I have found, which is becoming a mantra of mine, if you give you will receive. I always recommend that all my Agents pick an area to volunteer. I know many Realtors who have successful careers because they were involved with their children's school. I know other Realtors who volunteer in the hospital once a month. Others involve themselves with different charity organizations and yet others become a big brother or big sister. Some will work with homeless organizations and some will work with helping underprivileged find homes. The common thread for all these volunteering efforts is the fact that you will give back to the community and help someone. You receive the good feelings and good karma that go along with this work. Your heart and soul will be good and when this happens, everything is possible. Help and you will receive.

Chapter Twenty-One: FSBOs

The fact of the matter is that 90% of FSBOs end up using a Realtor. So how come all these other Realtors get all those FSBOs? Hard work and persistence comes to mind, but I have a better way. The reality is when you knock on a door trying to get the listing, the homeowner becomes tense and protective. They know you are trying to sell them something. Since we all know that success in Real Estate is helping people not selling them, help the FSBOs!

The first step is compiling all the forms used in transactions. This includes contracts, seller disclosures, lead based paint disclosure, homeowner disclosures and any other forms you think might be helpful. Then follow these simple steps:

a.   Knock on the door of the FSBO.

b.   Immediately introduce yourself. "Hi, I'm Mitch with Tropical Realty." (Their face at this point will look like, oh, no…not again). "I know that many Realtors have probably contacted you about listing you house, I'm not here to do that. I'm here to help you." (Now they will look at you strangely)

c.   Once you say that, they will become less defensive. From here you let them know that you have seen many FSBO transactions end up in a mess and you are offering your help in filling out contracts and to answer any questions they might have to ensure a smooth transaction. (Again they are looking at you strangely)

d.   The next question out of their mouths will be, "Why are you doing this?" The answer is simple: "I know that if I help you, and you know someone that might be looking to buy a home or sell a home in the future, you will remember that I was here to help. I work on referrals and this is how I do that."

e.   Once you have broken the ice, they will usually invite you into their home. This is your opportunity to give them suggestions to either stage or declutter the home. From here on it's all about building the relationship.

f.   Before you leave, give them a bunch of cards and ask them if anyone comes through the home that isn't represented by a Realtor, to give them your card. The last FSBO I used this strategy with never sold or listed their home, but she sent me two $850,000 Buyers!

g.   As you are leaving, it's important to let them know you work with a lot of Buyers and would it be okay if you brought them by to see the home. I say, "I work with a lot of Buyers. Would it be okay if I bring by anyone that might be interested? I do charge 3% if one of my Buyers buys. Is that okay?" I've never had anyone say no.

h.   Once you leave, go home and write a small note on a card reinforcing your desire to help them and send it along.

i.   If you were able to get their phone number, call in another week to see if they have any questions or stop by while you are in the neighborhood.

j.   The key, as in all sales, is follow up.

FSBOs are very easy to convert when their home has not sold for a month or so. They need the exposure. They need a Realtor. If you offer them help and use a soft sell approach, you will be the Realtor that wins them over.

Chapter Twenty-Two: Internet Marketing

Internet Marketing has been the new driving force in Real Estate over the last 10 years or so. There are many aspects to this, but in my opinion, the only action that works is direct marketing through Pay Per Click campaigns, which drives traffic to specific landing pages to capture leads. Most businesses look at a website as a brochure, which is unfortunate. A website should be a lead generating sales machine. It's all about traffic to your site and capturing leads to convert.

A.   **Facebook** – Facebook pages are great, but don't expect a tremendous amount of business from it. There is a lot of hype from NAR as well as a bunch of companies who are touting the benefits of Facebook and other Social Networking Sites. Unfortunately, nobody, at least to my knowledge, has turned this into a steady stream of business.

B.   **Facebook PPC** – Facebook Pay Per Click is great especially for valuation websites. Facebook offers the ability to place ads so they only show to specific demographics. For instance, when we are marketing our valuation sites, we simply put in the area code along with an age range of over 25 years old. The ad only shows to this group. You can do this to market specific organizations, companies, or any other group. It's very easy and very effective.

C.   **Blogging** – Blogging is another action that gets a lot of hype. However, it is extremely time consuming and may generate a sale or two per year.

D.   **SEO** – Search Engine Optimization is a great way to generate both traffic and capture leads to your site. However, (I say that a lot) to rank for a Real Estate site can take up to a year or more and be very costly in both time and-or money.

E.   **PPC Marketing** – Pay Per Click Marketing on Google and Bing are the most predictable means of marketing. If you spend X amount of dollars you will receive X amount of leads. It's fairly easy to do but it does take time and money to manage. In my Brokerage we use a company called Homegain for our Pay Per Click. You can go to www.HomegainBuyerLink.com to see if there is any traffic available in your area.

F.   **Lead Conversion** – No matter which form of Internet marketing you choose, it's all about Lead Conversion. Most Realtors convert less than 1% of their leads to sales. If you don't have any systems in place to convert leads, along with a strong CRM product, it's almost impossible to do this correctly.

G.   **Internet Brokerage** – I would always recommend, especially if you are a newer Agent or an Agent working hard but not able to generate the amount of leads to be successful, to join a Brokerage that understand Lead Conversion. It's a much more structured way of doing business, but in the end, it's almost always more successful than traditional Real Estate. Add both traditional and online together and you have a good foundation to grow your business.

In future chapters I concentrate a lot more on this subject. Internet Marketing has certainly changed the landscape of Real Estate Marketing. My Brokerage achieves over 50% of all sales from Internet and Lead Conversion programs.

Chapter Twenty-Three: Expired Listings

Very few Realtors work expired listings. The couple of Agents I know that work this market have done extremely well. The customer has already had their home listed so they want to sell. Sounds like a great market to me! Timeliness and how you approach the expired listing are crucial. You do have to check the *do not call* list to ensure they are not on the list. If so, you can knock on the door but you can't call them. We are going to assume they are not on the list.

The hardest part of working expired listings is making the call. At this point they are most likely frustrated that their home didn't sell and want to know why. Usually the reason a home doesn't sell is because of price. If a home is priced correctly, then it will usually sell. The key to the phone call is to be as upbeat and happy as possible. Remember to smile before you dial. Sounds cliché but it works wonders. It's very hard for someone on the other end to be mean or upset to someone that sounds so darn happy!

Before you dial, have your ammunition ready. You should read the expired listing and understand the finer points of the house. You should also do a CMA to find the "real" value of the house. They may not like what you tell them but they will have to respect your honesty. Once you have the ammunition, make the call.

    a.   Getting past hello is the hardest part. Since you are calling so cheerfully this shouldn't be a problem.

b.   After a little small talk, the first question you should ask is why do they think their home didn't sell. They will have a multitude of answers and it is very important that you listen to each one.

c.   Once you know the objections (their answers why their home didn't sell) you need to be able to answer each objection. The goal is to take whatever they perceived to be the reason they didn't sell their home and have a reason why you can make it happen.

d.   Once you have a conversation going, the next step is to get the appointment. Your goal during the entire conversation is to get the appointment. From there you already know the objections. Answer them and get the listing.

e.   In full disclosure, I have not worked Expired Listings in my career. I know that *expireds* are popular and a good source of potential listings. However, I have done extremely well without chasing the same customer that 50 other Realtors are chasing. *Expireds* just aren't my cup of tea!

Chapter Twenty-Four: Seminars

Informational Seminars are a tremendous means to gain business. One of my favorite seminars is a first time homebuyer program. There are always first time Homebuyers in the market that don't understand or know how to buy a home. Other seminars include Investment, Financing, Getting your Home Ready to Sell, Negotiating for a Home, etc. Anything educational will draw a crowd as well as the potential for many customers. There are different financing programs for first time Homebuyers, police, teachers, nurses and other community employees. Marketing should be done depending upon which audience you are trying to reach. For instance, first time home buying seminars should be marketed to renters in apartment buildings and homes. Teacher buying programs should be marketed to schools. Investment seminars might be marketed to businesses and the upper middle class.

At the seminar be sure to include the crowd into the conversation. Don't lecture for an hour and ask for questions. Ask questions from the beginning. You can always bring support in other Realtors, lenders or experts depending upon the flavor of the seminar. If you are not a good speaker, get someone you know to help you. Be sure to have a questionnaire for them to fill out. You need to find out what they are thinking and if they are serious now or later. Refreshments should be served as most seminars are after work and most people are hungry.

Marketing for seminars will obviously depend

on the seminar you are presenting. Here are two different approaches.

a) **First Time Home Buyer Seminar** – Marketing for this program is fairly simple. You can do a postcard mailing to every apartment complex where the rent is enough to pay for a home. You can also postcard market to homes that are non-owner occupied. We have had great success with this program and usually attract 20+ people and have sold 2-3 homes from each seminar.

b) **Hero's Financing Program** – This is one of my favorites. The Hero's program is offered by many lenders and is geared toward Police, Firefighters, Nurses and Teachers. Marketing is free as all you need to do is produce a marketing flyer and deliver it to every school, fire station, police station and hospital. Ask if they can either put a copy in every ones mailbox and or post it in the lunchroom. My results were about the same as for the First Time Home Buyer program. Regardless of what type of seminar you run, it's important to either have all the facts needed to present or bring in speakers. For instance, I didn't speak about the Hero's program. I had one of my lender partners speak. They also paid for all the refreshments and the room.

Chapter Twenty-Five: Education

The more you know the more you....well, know! You can never learn enough. I believe the more education you receive the better Realtor you will become. Your local board will offer a tremendous amount of education products and classes. Attend as many as possible.

I am often asked if someone should get this or that certification. I'm not a huge fan of certifications, but I am a very huge fan of the education you can learn by taking these classes. I don't think that most consumers have any idea what a GRI or CIPS means. However, the lessons from these classes to help grow your business are invaluable.

If you have not taken your post licensing class, take it as soon as possible. I would always suggest taking in classroom classes verse online, especially for post licensing. The lessons you will learn from other Realtors who took 2 years to take their test can prove very handy.

Chapter Twenty-Six: Work Full Time

This is easy. If you don't work 50+ hours per week you most likely won't be successful. Of course keep in mind that if you only sell 10 properties and they are all over $1 million, you won't have to work full time.

Most people have a hard time scheduling their time. The best way to be successful in time management is to organize your day on paper. Write down the hours of the day and plan a duty for that hour. If it is going to take you two hours, plan for it. This method will help you better time manage yourself.

Lists are a great way to accomplish your goals. I find that writing a list of things to do during the day does a few things. It places on paper what you need to do. As you start crossing things out that you have done, it gives you the sense of accomplishment from getting things done.

Finally, don't forget to look in the mirror. Success is your choice. You can go along and just get by or you can grab hold of this great opportunity and be successful. If you follow up, work your prospecting, are honest and ethical and work hard, you will be successful. It's up to you!

Chapter Twenty-Seven: Internet

One of the mysteries of small business marketing is the Internet. I have been involved with marketing on the Internet since 1996, and in Real Estate marketing on the Internet since 2001. The business principles are the same whether a Real Estate Brokerage or a Camera Shop. It really doesn't matter.

Much of this book consolidates information from training manuals I developed on the methods I have used to be successful in one of the nation's worst housing markets. It gives solutions to help *you* understand and grow your Internet program to generate hundreds of leads as well as to convert them to sales:

- **Internet marketing** – What is the best means of generating consistent traffic to your Website? I am an advocate of Pay Per Click marketing as it gives you complete control as well as predictability. However, PPC marketing can be extremely expensive and useless if you don't know how to use it properly.

- **Keywords** – Certain keywords and URLs will eventually result in higher rankings in the search engines. We help you find the best-possible keywords at the best-possible pricing. For instance, "Cocoa Beach Real Estate" is very expensive to market. However, "Coco Beach Real Estate" is very inexpensive with similar results.

- **Lead capture and landing pages** – Most businesses do not understand the importance or procedure of capturing leads off the Internet. Most businesses use their home page as the landing page when marketing on Internet. This is the worst strategy possible for lead conversion. We show you how the proper landing page converts more traffic to leads.

• **Lead Conversion** – How many times have you heard that Internet leads are horrible and a waste of time? Many companies are creating a ton of transactions from the Internet and you can too. We give you the step-by-step system (including our very own *40 Percent Rule*) to take your lead conversion to the next level!

One of my goals in this book is to help you, as a small businesses owner, to understand lead capture and conversion. However, no matter how good your systems are built, if you don't service your customer, you won't be a success.

I have worked for 30 years and owned 14 + companies. Sometimes I question why I don't just get a "regular" job like most people. I know I can earn a better-than-average income working for a company. But it's something I just can't do. My need to succeed keeps me driven at all times. Success has nothing to do with money; it has to do with accomplishing what I set out to do. With luck, accomplishing my goals usually means I earn a good living. I always figured money would come with accomplishment … and it does.

I have made many mistakes that have probably cost me millions of dollars. I never looked at those mistakes except as learning experiences, or tuition as my friend Mike calls it. Okay, it *did* take me some time to get over the failures before I appreciated their education benefit. In the end, however, I learned as much from my two failures as I did from my successes.

I have learned *you* have the power to succeed at whatever you desire. **Just do it!**

Chapter Twenty-Eight: The Truth About Internet Marketing

A successful business or salesperson must have an ongoing lead-generation program to sustain the business.

There are many aspects to being successful in business. You have to be honest. You have to be hard-working. You have to follow up. However, none of this matters if you don't have customers.

This means you need to generate leads. What good does it do your business if you possess these great qualities and ethics and you have no customers? **Leads are the essence of business development**. Leads are people who are interested in your product, and a percentage of these leads will eventually buy your product or service.

A successful business or salesperson must have an ongoing lead-generation program to sustain the business. I have seen so many businesses get caught up in fulfilling their sales that drop the ball on generating leads. Before they cut anything else, they cut their marketing budget.

How can you generate leads? Generating leads usually comes in the form of marketing. Marketing can be as simple as saying, "Hello," to someone in the grocery store to something as elaborate as a multimillion-dollar TV campaign. My favorite is the

Internet. If you work the Internet and have an effective Website, then collecting leads is extremely easy. Keep in mind, lead generation is not free. The key is to figure out the most cost-effective means to generate leads to build your business.

Truth be told, very few businesses around the country are actually making money with their Internet strategies. Usually the reason for their Internet failure is because they use tech people who have no idea how their industry works. Most of these companies include a lawyer and a tech guy who think they know what is best for all businesses.

What makes me an expert? I have been involved with Internet marketing since 1996. My first Internet company, Internet Community Concepts, actually had several companies under one roof: a dating service, chocolate company, flower company, advertising company and coupon company. With this company, the goal was to drive as many people to my Website and to gain revenues through radio station partnerships. It was a great company with excellent potential, but it was probably ahead of its time.

I was on track to sell it for a ridiculously large amount of money. Unfortunately, two months before closing, the market crashed, as did the deal and my company. However, I had learned the ins and outs of Internet marketing and how to drive people to my Websites. Each month, we were averaging more than 6,000,000 hits and 100,000+ unique visitors.

Once I made the commitment to get into the Real Estate industry, I knew I would add my knowledge of the Internet to my marketing program. My first year, I didn't do anything on the Internet, I just learned the business. By the middle of my second year I had added Internet marketing and started testing ideas. By the end of my third year I was fully engaged in Internet marketing and had so much business I hired three Buyers' Agents and a full-time assistant.

I now have 20 full-time Agents working 30+ leads I generate every day for them. The deal is, I will drive traffic and grab leads for them as long as they follow the systems I have designed to convert the leads. A few years ago with only 14 Agents and working only with Buyers, we were the #1 office out of more than 400 Real Estate offices in Brevard County, Florida.

The beauty of excelling in lead generation and lead capture is the fact that once you are set up and running, you can easily predict your business. Last year I was within 10% in transactions of my prediction. This is by design, not luck. Once you have great systems in place, you can track your conversion rate to predict exactly how many sales you will close.

For instance, I know that if I generate 30 leads a day, I will end up with approximately 22 sales for the month. After following our system many of our Agents are generating a much better conversion rate. (Our average the year we were #1 was 1 out of 24 leads.) Keep in mind that these include all leads; I call them raw leads. Our Agents are currently showing homes to 100+ different Buyers each month. Our sales are probably a reflection of the worst Real Estate market we have seen since the mid-1980s. However, I am very confident when the market comes back, we will be selling to half of those 100 Buyers and our sales will reach 50+ per month with only 20 Agents.

I'm giving you these stats so you understand

these tools and practices are what I use every day to build my Real Estate company. I practice what I preach.

I constantly look at different concepts and technologies to increase my business and help my Agents become successful. My business model is much different than most companies. I believe if I can make each of my Agents successful, we all win. If we all win, nobody ever leaves!

In fact, since we opened this office in March of 2005, we have only lost two Agents to another company. Unfortunately, I have had to let many go, and we did lose a couple who just didn't like the industry. All my Agents know that I have their best interests at heart and will do whatever it takes to make them successful. I would prefer to have 20 productive and happy Agents than 100 Agents with only 20 of them productive.

My goal is to help you build your business. I have learned a lot about the Internet over my years of being in Real Estate and Internet Community Concepts. I have spent hundreds of thousands of dollars on useless tools and with companies that told me they knew more than I knew. After all was said and done, they didn't!

Chapter Twenty-Nine: Internet Marketing is Imperative

There are many forms of online marketing. The key is to drive as much traffic as possible to your Website and then capture as many leads as possible. I look at it as a game. For instance, we usually get between a 10 percent and 16 percent capture rate, which means that up to 16 percent of the people who clicked on my site for the first time filled out one of our forms and became a lead. So out of 100 people on my site, I capture 12-16.

As I said, there are many opportunities to drive traffic to your site but we are only going to cover a few that are controllable. I prefer marketing that is measurable and predictable; I'm not a big believer in random Internet marketing. My practice is to use advertising to get a lead. That's it. That is the only purpose of my website, to capture and convert leads.

At this stage of the game our goal is not name recognition, it is lead generation. Name recognition is nice – it's the old-fashioned Real Estate way. I tried it for a year or two and if you do it well and have enough cash, you can build a long, successful career. However, most businesses do not have the money needed to truly be "branded." To do this correctly you need a steady campaign of TV, radio, newspaper, Internet banner ads and possibly billboards. I have done all these and they do get you brand recognition. What they don't get you is sales. Over time, they will build you a strong business. It will be costly, but it will work.

On the other hand, Internet advertising is the best means of direct marketing available to all businesses right now. For Real Estate, it's imperative. Every Agent and Broker I know has a Website. But do they have a Web marketing plan? Do they have any idea how to build an Internet marketing program that works?

My guess is 90 percent of businesses have no idea how to market their Websites. They believe all the companies saying, "Listen to us and you will be very successful and have the best Internet leads available." It's all rubbish. I have spent a small fortune checking out these companies to see if they work. I have bought banner ads. I have bought SEO placement services. I have bought keyword marketing services. I have bought Internet and postcard marketing services. I have bought so many of these products and services, my stomach aches when I think about all the money I blew.

Actually, you can do all this yourself. With the correct tools, advice and guidance, you can succeed with a winning Internet program. But you'd better be ready to be busy and you'd better have employees who will buy into the system. That's the key. If you do not believe in it and give it the time it needs to succeed, it will not work. It's an awesome new culture and a new attitude!

When the Internet began, marketing was limited mostly to banner ads. They were very expensive with very poor results. It was all so new that we were limited in our ability to really get out there over the Internet. If you didn't market on AOL, you were missing out on almost everyone who was online. I remember when they started doing text link advertising. We thought it was great!

Soon, the search engines – Google™ and Yahoo® – started offering advertising on their sites and eventually turned to keyword marketing. This allowed us to buy specific keywords that people would type. For instance, if someone typed in Melbourne Real Estate, I could buy an ad on their search page. We were all very excited as this changed the way we all would market on the Internet. We were now in control of our marketing budgets and could utilize the traffic the huge search engines would create.

The advent of the Internet also caused an interesting approach called affiliate marketing. Like offline businesses making private-label products, affiliates could use the tools someone else built to generate money for themselves. If you could think it, software guys and girls could build it. My first Website and site building system cost me $950,000. Yes, one of the problems with being a visionary is most of what I had thought up had never been done before. We had to create the tools to build what we wanted. In hindsight, I should have worked out an ownership deal on the tools they created for me.

Today, there are so many opportunities for small businesses to take advantage of this worldwide Internet market. Recently, one of our customers visited here from Ireland to buy a home. How else would I be able to market to customers in Ireland, England, France, Italy and more? Let's look at the most effective way to succeed with your personal Internet strategy.

Chapter Thirty: Keyword Marketing

Keyword marketing is the best current way of marketing your company. The "key" is that you can be as specific or as general as you wish. The bulk of all Internet marketing relies on picking keywords, so how do you do it?

It's actually very easy. Let's look at the easiest and probably most-used keywords. These will be specific to my area, but you can substitute your town(s) for mine.

Melbourne Real Estate
Melbourne Homes
Melbourne Lots
Melbourne Land
Melbourne Luxury Homes
Melbourne Mortgages
Melbourne Schools
Melbourne City Hall
Melbourne
Melbourne, FL
Melbourne, Florida

Currently I have more than 500 keywords over all my sites. Our office handles approximately 15 different cities in Brevard County on the east coast of Florida. If you use my example above with just those keywords across 15 cities, you see how your list can grow quickly. Keywords can be one word, a couple of words or a phrase. It can be anything industry-specific, such as Melbourne City Hall or Melbourne Schools. I use these types of keywords to draw in people who are trying to find out about my area.

The way to find out the best keywords is to go to Google Ad Words and use their tools to check the traffic each keyword will give you per month. They also will suggest tens of different keywords. It's all automated so you can play for hours trying to figure out the best words for your area.

No matter which form of Internet marketing you choose to do, you need to know the keywords that work best for you. Some of this effort will be trial and error. Some words you think will work well don't; others you don't think will work, do really well.

One more tidbit: keep in mind that searches are based on what consumers type into the search box. You may be surprised but some of my best keywords are misspelled words. They are always the least expensive to buy and are often very successful. For instance, one of my keywords is Cocoa Beach Real Estate but I also have Coco Beach Real Estate. Note the second spelling of "Cocoa." That keyword does extremely well for me and only costs me 10 cents per click.

Chapter Thirty-One: Pay-Per-Click

To pay per click or not ... that is the question! Pay Per Click (PPC) is one of the easiest, most controllable forms of Internet marketing. The best part is you are in complete control of how much you spend and you can target your marketing to be very specific in addition to being very general. You can be a small operation and appear to be huge. Depending on your budget, you can take over an entire area on the Internet or market just one neighborhood.

PPC is exactly what it says it is; you only pay for people who actually click the link going to your site. You can pay as little as 10 cents and as high as $20 per click. By the time you finish this chapter, you will know how to keep your costs low and your results high!

Who offers PPC? Nearly every major search engine offers a PPC model but the largest and most-used are Google's Adwords. They provide a huge amount of traffic, probably more than you will ever need. Here is an example taken from Yahoo after typing in "Merritt Island Real Estate":

• **Merritt Island Real Estate**
www.**troprealty.com** - Search for **Real Estate** in **Merritt Island** and surrounding areas...

• Mercedes Homes- Space Coast, Florida
www.**MercedesHomes.com** - Mercedes Homes builds homes in Brevard & Melbourne surrounding areas.

• **Merritt Island Real Estate**
www.**HomeFinderConnect.com** - See Homes For

Sale, MLS & More in the Melbourne/Palm Bay Area. Free.

WEB RESULTS

1. **Merritt Island Real Estate** - Melbourne **Real Estate** - Melbourne Beach **...**
Real Estate in **Merritt Island**, Melbourne, Indialantic, Melbourne Beach, Indian Harbor and Palm Bay.

The top two or three positions are sponsorship positions or PPC positions. Depending on your bid, you either will be in one of these spots on the first page or on other pages (offering less visibility). One of my company Websites, TropRealty.com, is #1. Below the sponsored listings you see the words WEB RESULTS. The listings after this are all there organically through search engine optimization (SEO).

PPC works on a bidding process. The highest bidder is the top position. The second-highest position is the next highest bidder and so on. (I have showed you the top three but the list of sponsors goes on and on.) Unfortunately, PPC systems don't tell you their customers' bids so it is a trial and error process. If you want to be number one it's fairly easy. You can *bid* substantially higher than everyone else. You will only *pay* one penny higher than the bid below you. An example:

Tropical Realty bids $2.35
Unknown Realty bids $1.35

In this scenario, you will only pay $1.36 for this click. Being number one will certainly drive more leads and traffic to your site. However, being number one is not necessarily the best place to be. I have found being #3 on the search engines will produce the best cost-per-click solution.

The tools on the search engines are not the easiest in the world to use. But you can figure them out after spending an hour or two playing with them. Learning them is not rocket science but it does take some time to be good at it.

The beauty of PPC is the control you have over your marketing. You can set your budget to $10 a day or $100 dollars per day or more. The choice is yours. You are sure to stay under your budget now with the advent of daily spending limits. The exciting PPC marketing result is that you will receive visitors to your site who are looking for your product or service. With PPC, you can do precision marketing – choosing your keywords to have total control.

The downside to PPC is that it changes daily and sometimes hourly. There are always other businesses trying to get higher than you in the search engine by trying to outbid you. That said, there is a little trick you can do to "kick" them out fairly quickly. The key is figuring out how close you are to your competition's bid. An example:

Your competition's bid = $2.00 (actually paying $1.26)

Your company's bid = $1.25 (actually paying $.76)

Your competition below your bid = $.75

The key to "kick" the top competition out is to up your bid to $1.99 in the above example. This way you are not outbidding him (or changing what you pay), just forcing the actual amount he is paying right up to his bid amount. Check out this next example to see how this affects your competition:

Your competition's bid = $2.00 (actually paying $2.00)

Your company's bid = $1.99 (actually paying $.76)

Your competition below your bid = $.75

As you can see, your costs per click did not change but your competitor's cost changed to $2 per click. This can get very expensive for him! It won't take long for him to walk away from that top position if the costs are too high and there are no sales from their marketing. This model works like a charm, especially when you really know what you are doing. The average small business owner doesn't really understand this Internet stuff!

Chapter Thirty-Two: Sales Companies & Third-Party Traffic

There are a few companies where you can buy site-specific traffic for Real Estate. Several companies are selling leads at a premium and sometimes at a discount.

I am not a big believer in lead-selling programs. I used a few of them several years ago and one sounded great until I actually paid. The reality is you are going to pay $30+ per lead, and you can do a better job on my own and more cheaply. Using my methods, your average cost per lead can be as low as $5 or even less, depending on your conversion rates.

Many companies tout their great-quality leads. I can tell you my experience based on the last company I tried, House.com. It promised me 10 leads at $50 per lead per month. I tried two months because the company claimed to call each lead and verify the individual was looking to buy or sell a home. Our office called all 20 leads over the two-month period. Not one person was the least bit interested in buying or selling a home. When I called and confronted the company, it said it only checked to make sure the phone number was a working phone number. That's a far cry from what they told me they were doing. In the end, after incredible efforts, I got my $1,000 refunded.

I have had no luck with the few lead-generation companies I've used, and the leads were no better than what I could generate myself. In fact, my leads have always been better than what I have bought from third parties.

Let's look at third-party traffic. I wasn't sold on this concept until I was approached by HomeGain.com. I don't want this to sound like a commercial for them, but I have been thoroughly satisfied with HomeGain's BuyerLink™ program (www.HomegainBuyerLink.com). This program sends traffic directly to the IDX page (lead capture page) on my Website. It is city-specific and you can buy as much or as little as you prefer. The best part is it's half the price of doing it yourself on Google and I don't have to invest any time to monitor my keywords.

A few facts since I have switched to HomeGain to receive my traffic:

• For the same price of using Google, I receive twice as much traffic

• My click-to-lead ratio changed from 7 percent to 8 percent, to between 12 percent and 16 percent on good days – that's more than double

• The lead quality from HomeGain is better, probably because the consumer clicks three times before even getting to my site

• I only pay for the traffic I receive, which is reported daily to me

No matter how you obtain your traffic, it's important to have the correct lead capture and conversion tools on your site. We will examine the best strategies to capture traffic visiting your site in the next section.

The key to companies that sell traffic is to **make sure the traffic is industry-related**. Do not buy anything from companies saying they will send 10,000 people to your site. There are hundreds of companies that will send you unrelated traffic and lots of it. All you will accomplish by that is obtaining a ton of useless leads, taking your time away from those leads that will generate sales.

To date, the only company that works for my Real Estate business is HomeGain and its BuyerLink program. Because of our ability to generate and convert leads, I have become somewhat of an Internet snob. Not with consumers of course, but with the companies telling me they are the best lead-generation company in the world and their leads are the best. I tell them to put their money where their mouth is. Give me leads for 30 days for free and let's see if they are any good. Of course, their answer to this is always … NO!

Isn't that a surprise!

Chapter Thirty-Three: A Successful Landing Page!

All your landing pages must be able to capture leads.

A landing page is the Web page consumers "land on" when they click from an online advertisement to get to your Website. One of the biggest mistakes of most small businesses is to have their landing page be their homepage – and nearly all of them do! They are expecting consumers to use their site and hoping they will click the "Contact Us" link to ask a question. Good luck with that strategy. If your goal is to offer free information and not to capture leads, go for it.

Remember the lifeblood of any business – especially a sales organization – is to generate leads. Without leads, you have no business. You can always go back to the old way of doing business through nonproductive marketing, but that can only go so far. That doesn't mean you can't do well, but in my experience that's why only one percent of the small businesses in the world actually make a good living. My systems and teachings are for the other 98 percent of you who don't understand how to generate business without spending a fortune on wasted advertising.

You can use multiple landing pages or you can have one landing page. **All your landing pages must have the ability to capture a lead**. I know that nearly every consumer who uses the Internet to search for homes is really *only* interested in looking at homes. This enables me to create my landing pages geared toward their needs. I have a landing page for every city we service. That page is the gateway to my county listings and my gateway to capture leads. It's the same way with products. Consumers are on the net every day looking for different products and services. Your landing pages should be geared to capture leads and we do this by being sure the consumer lands on the page that will help us do that best!

Over 90 percent of the Real Estate leads we capture at Tropical Realty of Suntree are from people registering to view home listings on our Website. You have to determine what it is on your site that consumers are willing to give you their information.

I constantly change our lead-capture form to increase my conversion rates. Currently we run from 12 percent on a slow day to 16 percent or higher on a good day. My goal is to get our capture rate at a consistent 20 percent. I don't know if that is possible because the fluctuations don't have any apparent reason.

Below is the form we currently use, specifically for Palm Bay, Florida. This is the page that comes up when someone on the Internet types the keyword *Palm Bay Real Estate* into the search engine and then clicks on us. A different keyword goes to a different landing page. All our IDX landing pages are the same with the exception of the city-specific content.

Welcome to your access to the **Merritt Island Real Estate**. Search for homes and condos in Merritt Island and surrounding areas. If you see anything that looks interesting to you, please don't hesitate to call or email. We are always here to help!

http://www.melbournehomesearch.com/Viera_and_

<u>Suntree Real Estate Home Search</u>

- **Search**
- **Recently Viewed**
- **Saved Items**

⊖ Main Search

> Condo
> Residential
> Townhouse
> Vacant Land

Min Beds:

[Any ▼]

Min Baths:

[Any ▼]

Min Price:

[Any ▼]

Max Price:

[Any ▼]

⊕ Other Options

Min Sq. Ft:

[Any ▼]

Max Sq. Ft:

[Any ▼]

Min Lot Size:

[   ] Acre(s)

Max Lot Size:

[   ] Acre(s)

MLS #

[   ]

Year Built:

[   ] [YYYY] or later

⊖Location

City:

```
Melbourne
Suntree
Viera
West Melbourne
```

(ctrl+click for multiple)

⊖

| doregister | thestaff@mitchrea | Viera_and_Suntre | QuickReg - 2 |

397951

Name:

Email:

Phone:

colony1internalter (Email will be used as Username ~ An Automated Password will be emailed to you.)

2

Do you have a ho

| Choose option ▼ | Would you like inf |

213 Do you have a home to sell?

214

Would you like info on financing?

| Choose option ▼ |

ABOUT SUNTREE:

Suntree is a planned community in Brevard County, just north of Melbourne. It's located near the center of the county, off I-95 between Rockledge and Melbourne. Suntree is a rapidly growing town that features nature trails, golf courses and the popular Brevard Zoo, home to over 400 animals! Close by you'll find the Indian River and the Atlantic Ocean where you can go fishing, boating, windsurfing, sailing and surfing. Or you can just relax on the beach, enjoying the Florida sun. Suntree real estate is highly sought after due to its affordable prices and access to great local schools.

ABOUT VIERA:

Viera was founded and created by a Czechoslovakian man and his family in 1912 from a small celery farm that grew into one of the world's largest and most respected family-owned agriculatural enterprises. Viera, from a Slovak word meaning "faith", is a planned community home to more than 19,000 residents and consisting of over 8000 homes. Viera features a vibrant town center, wildlife habitats, golf, conservation areas, miles of natural trails and recreational parks. And with easy access to the ocean and river, Viera is a place people love to live.

As you can see, we keep the form fairly simple but we do get them into the search mindset. I want them to start thinking about the buying process before they hit the search button. This is a work in progress and I will never be happy until I get 20 percent or more click-to-lead conversion rates!

One thing on the form has really done well for us are the questions at the bottom. Although the answers are not always accurate, they help us understand our customers a little more prior to talking to them. We know if someone responds that he is buying within a month, we'd better get on the phone with him immediately.

In addition, while we don't really consider ourselves a listing company, we receive many listings by asking if they have a home to sell. Even if Buyers are from a different area, we will help find them an Agent to work with for their sale. Then we receive a referral fee.

Finally, the financing question is great if you own a mortgage company like we do. But you also can partner with a mortgage company to work the mortgage leads for you. Check with other businesses that are non competing but target the same customers.

If you build proper landing pages, you will convert more traffic to leads. If nothing else, be sure all the online marketing links to your landing pages. Never be afraid to ask for people to register on your site to obtain what they are trying to obtain.

If Buyers want to view listings on my site, they are going to give me their names, e-mails and phone numbers. I can't tell you how many people appreciate that we are there to help. When we call our leads, they are almost always pleasant, fun and helpful. We hear, "I signed up for so many sites but you were the only ones that cared enough to call."

Chapter Thirty-Four: Convert Clicks to Leads— And Capture Them!

This is my favorite part of the job – increasing my click-to-lead conversion. Lead conversion is the number of leads you generate from the number of unique visitors coming to your site. Your lead capture rate must be maximized to keep your Internet costs reasonable.

I see so many people trying to use the Internet for their business who are wasting a lot of money. There was one I found in my area: a Brokerage with a search form you filled out to get to look at their listings. The problem was the listings were not where the link was going. I ended up going to a generic Website that pointed me to a different Website that in turn took me to another company's Website. In essence, they lost a customer.

The first rule is to be sure that all the pages on your site work correctly! Otherwise, it can get very expensive. In this case, the Broker is number one in the search-engine sponsored list and must be wondering why he is not getting any traffic! I hate seeing Agents and Brokers making these kinds of mistakes. So even though he is my competition, I had to call him and let him know.

Lead capture is vital for your Internet program and is one of the few measurable marketing campaigns you can use. By understanding and marketing lead capture, you can predict your business. I know by the number of leads I capture pretty much what my sales will be at the end of any month or year.

I have experimented with different landing pages and formats over the past several years to figure out which format gives me the best capture results. We know with our current form we receive 12 percent to 20 percent and sometimes as high as 25 percent conversion.

Not only is it important to capture the lead, it's important to have your customers come back to your site regularly. If you do a great job on capture and follow-up, they will always come back to your site. We receive sales from 3- and 4-year-old leads all the time because of our extensive follow-up systems by phone, Internet and e-mail. It all comes down to playing with different landing pages to see which give you the highest and best return for your advertising dollars.

To keep people coming back it's important to have tools such as saved listings, saved searches, new saved search and more. The content on your site is important. Once you have a customer who saves listings, you have a great shot at getting a new customer who will actually buy a home. The consumers that save listings are usually very serious about buying, and buying soon.

Chapter Thirty-Five: Lead Conversion

Sales is a numbers game. Success in sales has everything to do with how many leads you generate. Whoever generates the most leads has the best chance of being the most successful. Converting those leads to actual customers takes several steps.

- **CLASSIFYING LEADS**

The key to dealing with a large number of leads is the ability to classify each lead after your initial evaluation. Once you have received your lead, they need to be separated into categories:

1. **A lead with no phone number** – About 50 percent of leads captured on the Internet have no phone number attached or the wrong number. Put these leads into your monthly drip campaign. This means they receive your e-newsletter as well as an e-mail every 4-6 weeks simply saying you are just checking in to be sure they are receiving everything you sent. They also should receive updates of listings as they come on the market. By doing this, you know the prospect is receiving several e-mails monthly from you. This gives the impression you are working extremely hard for your prospect.

2. **A lead with a phone number** – The other 50 percent of leads have good phone numbers. These leads are also put into your monthly drip campaign via your e-mail system. When you talk with potential customers, it is important to determine their buying timeframe so you can place them in the correct call-back process. If the person is buying within 6 months,

put him into call-back every 2-3 weeks. If he is buying within 12 months, make monthly calls to him until he is 6 months away from buying. At that point, call every 2-3 weeks until he visits to view properties. If your customer is coming within a month, contact him at least once a week.

It is interesting to watch salespeople over the course of a year or two following a system. Many salespeople take a successful system and change it to make it easier or to fit it into their lifestyle. This is a huge mistake I see time and time again. The #1 change I see is the urgency in which the initial phone call is made.

Keep in mind your potential customers are doing their homework and researching nonstop until they make their purchase. Your initial phone call should be as quick as possible and NEVER more than **24 HOURS** after the lead is received. Every minute that goes by is another minute the lead starts to chill. After 24 hours your potential customer has already been on several other Websites. He who contacts the customer first usually wins!

After 4 years of following our lead system, we have learned a very valuable lesson: determine which leads are the hottest and work them the hardest. If you don't do a good job on your initial phone call to find out their timeframe to buy, you could be working hard on the wrong lead while another customer is out buying a home … without you. As much as we would like the Internet to do our entire job for us, we have learned that without the personal touch on top of great e-mail and follow-up campaigns, our conversion rate is much lower.

Why do some Agents do better with leads than others? I believe first and foremost they contact the lead very quickly. Once contacted, the Agent determines the buyer's timeframe and then puts the lead in the appropriate follow-up system. By organizing your leads from hottest to coldest, you are more likely to be working the leads that can potentially bring you a sale. If you want to take your game to the next level, you must be serious about developing that skill.

- **QUICK RESPONSE LEADS**

There are two types of leads: quick response leads (QRL) and long-term leads (LTL). QRLs should take priority over all other leads. These are potential customers looking to buy within 90 days. You should be all over these leads! When you have one, put it on the fast track and do the following:

- Call them at least once a week.
- Every few days send them a new list of everything that comes on the market. Do this even if they are getting this information automatically through the IDX on your Website. Remember, it's not always the *content* as it is the *contact*.
- Narrow down the MLS numbers of the homes they would be interested in seeing.
- Determine if they have talked with a mortgage company and try to get them pre-approved prior to showing them properties.
- In our office, we work as buyer Agents. If you are working as a buyer representative, explain what that means so they understand your loyalty to them.
- Educate them. We send a customer Q&A sheet as well as our Broker Guarantee Letter.

• Send maps, tidbits, a restaurant guide, golf leaflets, education information and anything else you think may be of interest to them.

The key on the QRLs is to overwhelm them with information and activity. Show them you are the best in the business and they will be satisfied with you.

• LONG-TERM LEADS

Long-term leads (LTLs) should be put on the back burner, but only to a degree. No pun intended! They still need an extremely aggressive follow-up campaign both by e-mail and by phone. However, with the LTL you allow the e-mail system to do most of your work.

Call them on a scheduled call-back system, which should be every 3-4 weeks if they are buying within the year, and every 6-8 weeks if it is more than a year. Our office receives many sales from leads more than 2 years old and sometimes more than 4 years old. You never know when Buyers are going to pull the trigger, so it's important to keep on top of them even as time goes by.

• KNOWING YOUR NUMBERS

This sounds so simple yet so many people in business don't follow this simple rule of thumb. Personally, I can't imagine running a business without knowing my numbers. With that said, I'm not the type of person who is totally anal about my numbers either, but I have found that knowing my numbers has helped me to grow my business very systematically and I know it will help you too!

Let's look at the simplest idea of knowing your numbers. We will take our program of generating leads from the Internet and converting them to sales. To understand what you need to do, you must first understand from which areas you must collect data to generate the numbers you need to know.

When working with the Internet there are five numbers I must know to help me understand and grow my business. I must know how much my cost is per click, what is my percentage of lead capture, how much my cost is per lead, how many leads it takes to close a sale and finally how much my cost is per sale. Once I know these three numbers I can then strategize how to grow my business.

Let's look at an example:

If I get 300 clicks through my pay per click advertising and it cost me $1 per click, it will cost me $300 for those 300 clicks. I know that if I have 300 clicks and I capture 10% of my click then I know for $300 I will capture 30 leads or $10 per lead. I know that we currently close 1 sale for every 25 leads we collect.

Therefore in this example, you can see that we going to spend $250 per sale. Does that make sense? Well it only makes sense financially if you are making more than $250 in a transaction.

Now let's look how we can take these numbers and increase business. We know that we have a few numbers here that influence our outcome. For instance we know that our lead capture rate is 10%. We also know that our lead closing percentage is 4%. So if everything else stays the same but we increase our capture rate and closing rate, what will happen? Yes, our cost per sale goes down and therefore we end up with more cash in our pockets! This is how I have grown my business from just myself and three Agents to 30 Agents and growing over the past 4 years. But what did I do to increase my business?

It was really very easy. At the time I had an 8% capture rate and a 2% close rate. I realized that if I could increase either of those numbers, I would instantly increase my business. I also realized that if I didn't increase either of those numbers but increased my monthly clicks (traffic to my site) I would also increase my business.

At the time I decided to work on all three. I increased my monthly spending which automatically increased my lead flow and, therefore, my sales. However, I didn't want to just throw money in marketing to increase my business. I wanted to increase my sales while hopefully lowering my costs. My goal was to work on increasing my capture rate. I knew if I could increase my capture rate alone that would increase the number of leads...which would increase my sales. So let's look at what an increased capture rate does to our numbers.

When I first started my team these were my numbers (not my actual numbers but actual percentages):

Cost per click - $1
Capture Rate – 8%
Number of Clicks – 1,000
Number of leads – 80
Cost per lead - $12.50 per lead
Number of Leads per sale – 52
Cost per sale – $650.00

In this scenario, only 1 ½ sales resulted from those 80 leads.

At the time our average sale was around $200k or $3,000 in commission. Would you spend $650 to earn $3,000? To me, every day of the week! But of course I wanted better. So let's change a couple of numbers and see what type of affect this would have on the business.

   Cost per click - $1
   Capture Rate – 12%
   Number of Clicks – 1,000
   Number of leads – 120
   Cost per lead - $8.33 per lead
   Number of Leads per sale – 35
   Cost per sale – $291.67

   In this scenario we would have had 3.5 sales for 120 leads with the same amount of money spent on marketing.

   Can you see what happened here? We increased our lead capture by 4% and lowered our lead conversion rate to 1 out of 35 leads, and look what it did with our numbers. We spent the same amount of money but it resulted in a cost per sale of now only $291.67, a lead cost of only $8.33. We also generated 2 more sales per month.

   So basically if we use the same $200k per sale, we would have spent $1,000 to generate over $9,000 in commissions…again a no brainer!

   Hopefully you are starting to understand the power of knowing your numbers.

   Now let's take it one step further by increasing our clicks. This will show you how I really started growing the company.

   Cost per click - $1
   Capture Rate – 12%
   Number of Clicks – 10,000
   Number of leads – 1200

Cost per lead - $8.33 per lead
Number of Leads per sale – 30
Cost per sale – $249.90

In this scenario we would have generated 40 sales and lowered cost to $249.90. But we did increase spending by $9,000. However, if we go back to our initial commission per sale of $3,000, we would have generated $120,000 in commissions for a cost of only $10,000.

Is this starting to make sense? It's actually very easy to grow your business once you know your numbers. The same is true in running your business for all your expenses. It's so important to have a clue on how much money it costs you to run your business. I have been guilty myself of letting my spending get away with me.

Once a quarter or so I have to sit down and reel myself in so I don't spend too much money. I tend to like to try different things that cost money…I always end up with the same findings. It's just more cost effective to continue to run my marketing through the Internet and follow my numbers. They have not led me wrong yet.

As with everything, getting a handle on these numbers takes practice. Things fluctuate all the time. Our lead capture can be as high as 16% and as low as 10%. I haven't figured out how to make it consistent. I have figured out that as long as I figure my numbers on the low end, I will do fine! Understand your numbers and you will soon understand the magic of growing your business!

Chapter Thirty-Six: Lead Conversion Administrator--LCA

After almost two years of trial-and-error, we have finally figured out how to turn an LCA into a profitable portion of our business. In the end, we have determined that for as important as the first phone call is in the lead conversion process, the subsequent follow up calls are just as, if not more, important. Before getting into the current process we are using, let's talk for a few minutes about how the program has evolved over the past two years.

The first part of moving forward with the LCA program was to decide which Agents to put into this system. I had several Agents at this time that were not doing as well as I would like. I decided that their weakness was phone calls and I would have the LCAs work with these Agents. Good thought, but bad idea. I will elaborate more on this in a bit.

Our initial thought for the LCA was to have her make the first phone calls for 5 Agents. Based on the notion that first calls needed to be made as quickly as possible, it made sense to me to have her make this call.

This would insure, from my point of view, that all calls were being made, which would increase our lead conversion rate. It was up to the Agents to make the follow up calls.

From the beginning, it seemed to as if the program was taking traction. I hired an additional LCA within a month. I noticed a small up tick in sales, but not enough yet to justify the salaries I was paying out. Within a few months, one of the LCAs realized that with all the great calls she was getting, she would rather be an Agent. I decided at that point to not add another LCA into the picture, but work with the one LCA to perfect the process.

In June of 2008, we added our 100MPH software to the mix, which helped the LCA as well as my Agents become more organized. Sales increased shortly thereafter by about 20%. I attributed this to the addition of our software. The LCA position was turning more into an admin position and got away from making the quantity of phone calls needed for this program to be successful. I had thought many times to terminate the program, but I knew that it would work. I just had to figure out the right formula.

By December of 2008, the LCA and I decided that the current execution of this position wasn't working. The Agents under our LCA program did not increase their sales. I was disappointed, as was the LCA. After brainstorming for a bit, we decided to take all the Agents currently using this program off the program. Instead of having our weaker Agents on the program, we would have some of our stronger Agents on it. It became apparent that weaker Agents, unless willing to put in the amount of work needed to be successful, were not going to succeed in my system or any other system. It really comes down to work ethic and no matter how good your systems are, if your Agents aren't buying into the system and are not willing to work hard, you are bound to fail.

Even though it wasn't working great, it was helping my busy Agents be more productive. Finally, we were seeing some positive results. As little as the increased production was, it was a sign that I was on the right track. I knew I still had changes to make, but at least I became more optimistic. I have always known that the phone call aspect of Internet Lead Conversion is vital. Without developing a solid phone call follow up strategy along with a strong relevant drip campaign, Internet leads are tough to convert. The combination though is very strong and we were close to a breakthrough. At this point we were converting leads at 1 sale out of 24 leads. Not bad, but I still knew we could do better. Sometime around March, after meeting again with my LCA and her Agents, we decided that the LCA position would be better at making all the follow up calls, and letting the Agents make the first calls. The reality was we were losing a ton of sales because the Agents were not doing a good job following up on their leads.

From January through August 2009, I had interviewed a bunch of Agents for the LCA position. I was very frustrated, as I couldn't find even one Agent that had the work ethic and desire needed to fulfill this position. I was at a loss on how to find the right people for the job. Up until August, I had been sending out emails to every Realtor in the county and I had had many calls and many interviews. There wasn't one person I would have hired at this point. I was concerned that even if I was able to really grow this program, that I would have trouble hiring the right people for the job. I decided it was worth a try for the LCA program. My first ad I had 10 responses and would have hired 4 of the candidates I interviewed.

I hired a new LCA at the beginning of October

with our current LCA training her. I assigned the next 5 best Agents to work with the new LCA. I wasn't totally sold on our system yet, so making this commitment of hiring another LCA was a little scary!

At the same time that the new LCA was being trained, I was still trying to figure out how to improve on the system. At this point, it wasn't a matter of making the calls, it was figuring out who were the best leads to call. Our software offers us the ability to really break down our leads to find the best leads. For instance, I can see who has been on the site the past 24 or more hours. I can also search by price range, area code and whether or not a lead confirmed their email address. With these tools at our fingertips, I realized that we could really drill down to find our most active leads. However, even though we had this capability, we were still not getting the results I wanted and needed to really be excited about this program.

I struggled with this program for a couple more weeks and was in and out of the software trying to find the solution. As with most things, I knew it would just jump at me when I was ready to learn it. And it did. I found that the LCAs were only contacting about 3 – 5 leads per week and spending a ton of time doing admin work for the agents including saving new searches and writing very long informative notes to the Agents. It was at that point I realized I was doing it all wrong. I immediately met with my LCAs the following morning and made a drastic change. They were no longer to do any admin work for the Agents and they were required to contact at least 3 leads per day for each Agent, 5 days per week. At first the LCAs and the Agents didn't take too well to this. The LCAs thought I didn't think they were working hard enough and the Agents didn't want to do the extra admin work themselves.

I reminded all of them that the purpose of the LCA position was to contact leads and figure out who is going to buy and when they are planning on buying. They all agreed…weren't happy, but agreed.

This was where it started to get exciting. We saw immediate results. Of course, the downside was we were now in the middle of November with Thanksgiving and Christmas right around the corner, our slowest three months each year. I was so excited that finally, after two years of trial-and-error, we had figured out the right formula, the right system. The outlook for 2010 was looking very promising.

Over the next few years the system worked well. We continued to keep our lead conversion between 3.5% and 4.5% of our raw leads. So let's fast forward to 2014. At the beginning of 2014 our two LCAs had 15 Agents each. We continued to keep our lead conversion between 3.5% and 4.5% of our raw leads. In January, we hired our third LCA and increased our Agents on leads to 40. Our first quarter was again successful, but I kept saying to myself, "I'm missing something…I just know I'm missing something."

Many meetings later after really understanding the weakest link in the lead conversion process, we have made yet more changes. The weakest part of lead conversion for any brokerage is the lack of first calls and follow-up calls made by any Agent. We know that if Agents call one time, they will get ahold of 35% of the leads. If they have called four times, that number jumps to 80%. However, most Agents will only call once. Even with the LCA program and a current database of 52,000+ leads, it's impossible for the LCAs to keep in touch with the most active leads. The LCAs are constantly calling behind the Agents to try to get hold of all the leads. The result of adding more Agents and more leads did not produce more sales. It actually created more strain on the LCA system. I finally had to make a change that I had wanted to make for quite some time but wasn't quite ready to spend the money.

Here is a fact: we lose an average of 300-400 sales per year. In 2010, I tracked how many of our leads told us "thank you, but we've already bought a house". Even with our LCA program working well, we still couldn't stay on top of all our leads. With this said, we decided to hire two new members to our Lead Conversion Team. First, we have hired a Search Admin (SA) whose only job is to make sure that all searches are done for each lead. Most of our Agents weren't doing new searches for leads with bad or no phone numbers. The SA s first job was to go back a year and do a new search for all leads with no or bad phone numbers. We saw an immediate uptick and people opening their emails and responding to our Agents. Second, we hired a First Call Admin (FCA). The FCA position is required to make the first call to every new lead that comes in within the first 10 minutes or less. Obviously, this can't happen all the time with leads registering at night. The following are the job descriptions and responsibilities of our LCAs, SA, FCA, and Agents.

Lead Conversion Department Structure and Lead Flow

Employee by Job Description

1. **LCA - Lead Conversion** Agents - Responsible for calling leads daily based on different groups and timing. LCAs are our main contact throughout the nurturing process.

2. **SA - Search Agent** - This position is responsible for investigating, verifying, and setting each search, both on new leads and on existing leads, when given information from the FCA or LCAs to make changes.

3. **FCA - First Call Agent** - This position is required to call all new leads and other call projects give by LCA. Required to call all property inquiries and follow behind to identify if they were worked, then notifying the appropriate LCA if they were not.

Lead Flow Process

Purpose - To ensure that all leads are set up in correct saved searches, first calls are made until contact, and leads are effectively nurtured until leads are ready to buy.

1. Lead registers and is assigned to Agent

2. Every day, first thing, FCA makes the first call to all new leads from the previous day; (Identifying themself as part of the agent's team – doing this will set the stage for working with a team. Example: "Hi, this is Liz from the Tom Jones Real Estate Team...") thanks them for registering on the website; verifies the email and telephone number; and goes over the saved search. If the search needs to be adjusted, it will be sent to the SA to revamp and resend new search. At the end of the conversations, the FCA will inform the lead that the agent or the agent's assistant will be contacting them next week, giving them time to view the listings and to see if they are happy with what has been set up, unless

they need immediate assistance, in which case we connect them with an agent that day.

3.   Search Agent works all 'No or Bad Phone Number' (NBPN) new leads from previous day at the beginning of the day. SA will complete any new searches that are identified from FCA, making contact with the new leads, and anything the LCAs send. SA will check at the end of the day to work any new leads that the FCA was not able to reach. SA will work on older date ranges or special projects to adjust searches or to complete any specialty searches.

4.   FCA will continue to call until contact is made - Once contact is made, FCA will put the lead into the AL group, updating the notes accordingly.

5.   LCAs will pull new leads that the FCA and the SA have worked and put them into the AL group. They will call to check on the searches and to see if the customers are happy with what we have set up for them. At this point, the LCAs will try to determine a timeframe that the lead is planning to purchase within.

6.   Each LCA will also create call lists for the FCA to call all the new leads that have not been reached an additional 2-6 times. Once they are reached, we will follow the same process.

7.   Once the LCA has identified that the lead is coming to within 60 days of purchase, the lead will be turned over to the agent. The LCA will monitor to be sure follow-up is completed. If not, the LCA will transfer the lead to another Agent, giving the next Agent a little time to try and build the relationship with the lead.

8.   On property inquiries, FCA will call and let the lead know that we received their request, but that the Agent is out in the field and will get back to them within 24hrs, unless they need immediate assistance. Then we can connect them with an Agent right away. If the Agent isn't available, the lead will be transferred. If the Agent doesn't respond to the customer within 24 hours, the lead will be transferred.

Below is the form that we use to insure we ask all the right questions.

Customize this for your market. This is our first fact finding form we use to help us better find our potential customer's needs.

Lead Real Estate Pre-Qualification Sheet

Complete this form for every customer you talk with on the phone or by email. This will allow you to better help your customers with their search and also improve your time management. Circle the correct answer or fill in the blank.

(Customer), as a Home Buying Consultant, we do things a little different than most Real Estate Companies. In order to give you the best advice possible, I have a few questions I would like to ask you.

Ok, here we go!

☐ Firstly, are you currently working with a Realtor? Yes or No?

☐ When are you going to be moving to the area? – 1 Month, 3

Months, 6 Months, 1 year +

☐ Is this going to be a primary, vacation or retirement home OR

Why have you decided to move to the area at this time?

_____

_____

☐ If out of state: When do you plan on coming down to look at homes?

_____

☐ Tell me a little about the home you are looking to buy. How many bedrooms, baths, sq. ft etc. What would be your ideal home?

_____

_____

_____

_____

_____

☐ From what I see your price range is _____ to _____ Is that correct?
If no, write price range _____ to
_____.

☐ Do you have a home to sell prior to your moving here? Yes or No

☐ Have you been to Brevard County before? Yes or No

☐ How did you hear about Brevard County?

_____

_____

_____

☐ Have you already talked with a Mortgage Broker or Lender? Yes or No.

If No, would you like me to have our preferred lender give you a call? Yes or No

☐ Tell me a little about the lifestyle you would like to live…do you have children, play golf, fish, surf? What do you plan on doing when you get here?

_____

☐ If Yes to Children, are they school aged?

☐ How familiar are you with the Real Estate market in Brevard County?

Chapter Thirty-Seven: Follow-Up, Follow-Up, Follow-Up

This is lead conversion. This is sales. Without follow-up, you may as well leave the business and get a regular job. How boring!

We have talked about when to make the phone calls. During these phone calls, it's imperative you build trust and bond with your customer. This is one of those points separating the successful from the "just okay" Agents. Try to accomplish the following on your phone calls:

1. **Use humor** as much as possible during your phone calls. Laughter is the best medicine and can break down the salesman/customer barrier. Humor can build trust, rather than making customers feel like you are trying to "sell" them.

2. **Educate your customers.** Let them know exactly what you will be doing and how you will be doing it. They need to understand you will give them 150 percent and you expect them to be loyal to you too. Try to find out sooner rather than later if they are working with multiple Agents. We see it all the time and the sooner you break the resistance, the sooner they will stop working with other Agents. Educate your customer on how you deal with **new construction** and with **FSBOs**. Let them know that if they are driving around and see a home they like, they should contact you so you can get them into the house. And because in our office we work as **Buyer Agents**, we reinforce to

the customer that we are representing them and looking out for their best interests.

3. **Accurate information.** If your customer is looking for specific information, this is when accuracy of content is very important. Never answer a question when you really don't know the answer. Once they find out you weren't telling the truth, you can say goodbye to them. Find out the information or get them the phone numbers relevant to their question as quickly as possible. Remember, service is what is going to keep your customer by your side through the entire process.

4. **Listen.** It's very important you listen to your customers' needs. Just because they submitted one thing on their lead sheet doesn't mean that is all they are looking to buy. Be sure when you get off the phone you send them a new list of properties and adjust their criteria in the prospecting tool.

By becoming excellent at follow up, you will become excellent in growing your business. Great follow-up will produce great results!

Chapter Thirty-Eight: The 40 Percent Rule

My office has been working leads for several years. We have figured out certain trends – but none more important than the activity actually being done by our prospects. I have analyzed our customers and realized approximately **40 percent** of our prospects are actually using our system. This means they are either saving listings or going into their listing cart to see listings sent to them.

So what is the 40 Percent Rule? It is the ability to identify those 40 percent in your database who are currently using the system. The other 60 percent most likely are never going to buy anything from you or our company. In fact, the chances are they are never going to buy anything from anyone!

You see, one of the biggest complaints I get is there are just too many leads to follow up. (By the way, it's a good complaint.) It's understandable, since each year we receive hundreds of new leads. To me, the best way to becoming more successful is to devote most of your time on efforts that are going to generate customers and sales for you. It's really very simple. If you look at your prospect manager, you will see who has been on the system on a regular basis. These are the most important people in your system.

So according to my research, if you have 1,000 leads in your system, you should have approximately 400 people who are actively looking to buy a home. (Most of our Agents actually have that many leads.) Just think, if you can help just 10 percent of those people buy a home, you have 40 sales or have done approximately $8,600,000 in volume. Wow, that's amazing! What if you helped just 15 percent or 20 percent of those leads in a year? Can you see where I am going with this?

You have 40 percent of your leads actively looking for a home. If potential customers are checking all their updates and actively looking for a home, then a minimum of 10 percent of them will buy a home this year. So while you are figuring out how to get more business, just look at your computer. There are plenty of people looking to buy right now!

Chapter Thirty-Nine: Partnerships to Drive Traffic

While I was building my Internet company back in the 1990s, I figured out I could generate more traffic to my Websites if I could private-label my products. Private labeling is the ability to have another company resell your products with their own branding, but with you fulfilling the back end. Another name for this is affiliate marketing. To me it's a no-brainer, and my results have been outstanding. Let me give you an example.

We have a deal with www.BrevardCounty.com, which has received 30,000 unique visitors per month. The company markets the ability to search homes under the Brevard County Real Estate section of its site. Our deal is very simple. We provide the Real Estate search engine through our IDX, and all the leads that come to us will be copied to them. It's a win/win situation.

Our Website receives additional traffic and BrevardCounty.com has access to a tool to capture names and e-mail addresses for their business. We also send our 28,000+ database of Buyers a link to the *Discover Brevard* magazine, which does not have any other Real Estate marketing. Our goal is to capture 10 percent of their traffic to our IDX. Hopefully, 20 percent of those coming to the search page will become leads. By accomplishing this, we should see a 20 percent increase in our lead flow.

We are always looking for partnerships around

the county and the nation.

I built my entire Internet Company on affiliate marketing. At the time, I had my online dating service and all the content we provided. We would contact radio groups and other groups that had or had the potential to have a lot of traffic. Our model was simple: give the media groups additional content along with products so that we could share in the revenue. Our product line was our dating service, a couponing service, things to do listings platform, a candy store, flower store and an online advertising platform. All our products appeared to be our partner's products. They did the marketing and we did the fulfillment. This of course doesn't work for all businesses, but any business that is retail driven can accomplish the same results.

Chapter Forty: Listening to and Evaluating Your Customer

An important aspect of converting your leads to sales is the ability to listen to and evaluate your customer. On a daily basis I hear people talking about this customer or that customer who wants to be shown 100 homes in one day! How are you going to do that while trying to help the many other customers you are working with?

A key to success in Real Estate is the ability to generate customers, as well as to know which customers are just looking and which ones are serious. Agents will spend a significant time working hard for the wrong customer, only to find the right customer went somewhere else. How do you figure out which is the right customer you should invest your time and effort into? You listen!

LISTENING IS KEY

I can't stress this enough: are you listening to your customer? Remember the 40 Percent Rule. Our goal is to find 10 percent of the 40 percent who are willing and able to buy a home this year. To do this, it's extremely important to implement effective listening skills.

Example: Your customer has a home to sell and he wants to look at 20 homes today and 20 homes tomorrow. His home is not currently on the market and he needs to sell it before he can think about buying anything.

Answer: You would be spending 2 days of your time and gas driving around with a customer who may buy in the future but is definitely not buying at this time.

To be effective in sales you must learn to listen and evaluate your customers. You must be able to pick out the lookers from the Buyers. This isn't always easy, but it's an area where you must always strive to be better.

Here are phrases that "lookers" use:

"I'm not in a real hurry. We are just thinking about buying sometime in the future and want to see what's out there."

"I have a house to sell, which I will put on the market if I find anything I like."

"I have to sell my house before I can buy anything." (but it's not on the market yet)

"I have to sell my house; it's currently listed but nobody has shown it in months."

"We are coming in on vacation and want to spend a day looking at houses to see if we want to move to the area."

Understanding your leads is one of the keys to success in lead conversion. If you don't take control of your customers, they will take control of you. Once that happens, it becomes difficult to give your serious Buyers the time and effort to help them purchase their homes.

I am not telling you to ignore these lookers, because at some point they may become Buyers. When I have new potential customers coming to the area and I know they are not buying today, I will spend 4 hours with them. I will show them a few homes, but more importantly I will show them a few *areas*. As we all know, if they don't know the area where they want to live, finding them a home will prove difficult.

Spend some time with them, explain to them that you deal with many Buyers and this is the process. Show them one home or two or four. Keep in mind most consumers don't know the purchase process, especially the process of working with a Real Estate professional. You set the rules, you take control. Then you will be able to put most of your efforts toward your serious customers. Educate your buyer on the area and on how your market compares to other markets. After all, you are the expert!

Evaluating Your Customer

Okay, so you have listened to your customers' needs and it's time to make some hard decisions. You know that it's important to figure out which customers are just looking for a tour of the area and homes for the fun of it, and others who are serious about buying.

This is something you should know prior to meeting with your customers. If have been listening well and asking the correct questions, you should know your customer's motivation. It's important that you ask them if they are buying or just doing their research.

You can accomplish this by simply asking. Let's talk about some of the questions you should be asking when first talking with your customer.

1. Are you buying a primary residence or a second home?

2. When do you want to move into your new

home?

    3. Why are you moving?

    4. Do you have a home to sell before you can buy?

    Let's look at those four key questions first.

    Question 1 tells me that someone who is looking for a primary home is more apt to buy quicker than someone looking to buy a vacation home or second home. Of course there are also many exceptions to this rule so it's important that you judge by all four of these questions not just the one question.

    Question 2 helps to arm you with the ability to prioritize your customers.

    Obviously, someone who is looking to buy in a month is a lot stronger than someone who is looking to buy in a year or so. By stronger we mean quicker. They are more likely to buy quicker than others who say they won't buy for a year.

    Question 3 is self explanatory. Knowing why they are moving will help you to understand their motivations for moving.

    Question 4 is going to let you know if anything is preventing your customer from buying when they are here to look.

    All four of these questions deal with motivation. Why and when are they moving? By understanding their motivation, you have a much better ability to place them in the order of priority. Remember, that is our goal. It's imperative to work with the customers that are most likely to buy.

    Let's look at these in a hypothetical situation.

    Example: I've been talking on the phone with this lady and I want to find out as much as possible about her motivation to buy. We will call her Lisa.

Mitch: Lisa, so I can better prepare myself for your visit, I have a few questions for you.

First, are you buying this home as a primary residence or is this going to be a vacation home for you?

Lisa: I'm buying it as my primary residence. My husband is being transferred to (your city).

Lisa just answered two of my questions because now we know it's their primary residence and their motivation for moving is her husband's job transfer. No need to ask question #3.

Mitch: Great, we work with relocations all the time since 80% of our business comes from out of state. When are you looking to move into your new home?

Lisa: Pretty quickly. He is being transferred in the next 60 days so time is pretty crucial.

Mitch: Well, I'm glad I can help you. When are you coming down to look?

Lisa: We will be down next week.

Mitch: One last question. Do you have a home to sell? As you know, if you have a home to sell it will affect how we look at homes.

Lisa: No, we don't have a home to sell.

As you can see with this example, she is a high priority. These are my favorite types of customers because their goals and needs are clearly defined. Lisa would jump to the top of my priority list.

Let's look at another example:

Example: I've been talking to Robert for a couple of months.

Robert: I'm thinking we are going to be in (your area) next month. We are taking the kids to that amusement park with the big mouse.

Mitch: That's great! I'm looking forward to meeting you. I have a few questions for you so I can best plan your visit to maximize your time.

Robert: No problem. It's okay that we will have the kids with us, right?

Mitch: Of course, it is! I'm sure I might have asked you these questions in our past conversations, but I want to make sure I got it right. Firstly, are you buying this home as your primary home or a vacation home?

Robert: This is going to be our vacation home and then hopefully our retirement home some day.

Mitch: That's a great plan. I deal with a lot of customers that do the exact same thing.

Why not buy your retirement home while you can afford it! When are you guys looking to buy?

Robert: We aren't sure right now. We know we want to buy, but we want to make sure that (your city) is the one we want to move to. After all, there are so many choices in (your state).

Mitch: There sure is. I will tell you that I moved down here from Boston because it was the least expensive waterfront area in Florida and it is less crowded. If I wanted crowds I would have stayed in Boston! So why have you decided to make the move now?

Robert: Like I said, we are just in the researching stage and aren't sure exactly when we are going to buy. I do know that the prices are the best they have been in a long time so I don't want to wait too long.

Mitch: Many would say this is the best time we

have had to buy in the past few years. Prices are down and interest rates remain low. It's a great time to take advantage of both these factors. Do you guys have to sell a home to buy?

Robert: No, we are going to keep our current home and buy this as a vacation home. We don't own any other property.

Mitch: Great. Some people need to sell another piece of property to buy their vacation-retirement homes.

This is more the typical customer. They are not in a hurry but if they found the right home they might act on it. Of course, there is more to this conversation as far as questions to ask with regard to their needs.

How would you rate this customer on a scale of 1 – 10? My goal for you is to be able to take 10 customers and prioritize them in order between 1 to 10, with 1 being the most important and 10 being the least important. Robert, in the above example is going to buy a home at some point. However, while he is down here he will be distracted by the family and the other attractions that his family really wants to do.

Believe me, there aren't many kids that are going to want to go look at homes. The chances of him buying right now are slim, but there is a possibility. I would rate Robert right around 7 or so. Since they are only going to be available for a day or two, I would schedule half a dozen homes for the first morning to give them an idea of what their money will buy. Even though they have been looking online, it's not the same as going to the homes themselves. At the end of that first day, I would ask them what the liked and disliked about the homes they just viewed. I would also ask if he thought he would like to make an offer on any of them. By asking this question you will find out if he is really motivated or just interested in looking at this time.

Summary

One of the hardest aspects of Real Estate is keeping organized, following up and making sure you are helping your most motivated buyer at any given time. Once you start asking the right questions, it will become very clear on who you should help the most in the present. We have all made the mistake of neglecting one customer because we were so busy with other customers. How many times has that customer bought a home through another Agent? Was it because you were not available when they needed you? Was it because you were too busy taking care of the wrong person?

Let's get something straight though. You don't want to neglect any of your customers. You want to make sure you offer tremendous customer service with all the customers you help. The key is understanding which customers are your hottest and which customers are not. Once you know your priority list, it's important that you devote the majority of your time to the top 4 or 5. However, be sure to provide as much as possible for the other 5 or 6. It's very possible that they are going to buy at some point or another.

Hopefully, this will help you become more astute at prioritizing your customers so you can be the most efficient for both your customers and yourself! Is it possible you may lose a customer here and there? Yes, that is definitely a possibility. You may lose a customer or two along the way, but you will certainly make up for that by being a better Realtor for the customers who need help now.

Chapter Forty-One: Color Codes

Lead Assignment Letter

Email Subject Line: Thank you for using web address

> Initial Drip: 30 Min
> Group Assignment: Search MLS
> Assigned Status: Prospect
> Hi {contactfirst}!
> Thank you for taking the time to use our website

at web address.

My name is {name} and I will be contacting you shortly to discuss your Real Estate needs as well as sending you a list of properties fitting your criteria. If you have any questions in the meantime, feel free to contact me at {phone1} or Email {email1}.

I have added your name to our update system, which will notify you of any new listings and/or changes in listings fitting your criteria. The notification will have **County** Property Listings in the subject line. The Listing updates will be coming from {email1} and may be sent to your spam folder. Please remember to check your spam folder.

If you have any Real Estate questions, or would like to view any listings, please don't hesitate to contact me at {phone1}. I can show you ANY property listing in **County**!

Again, thank you and I look forward to helping you!

Have a great day!

{staffsignature}
"You are receiving this email as you either subscribed to one of our websites at or were added by one of our Agents."

First List of Properties
Email Subject Line: County Property Listings
Initial Drip: 60 Min
Group Assignment: Search MLS (and any other group you'd like)
Assigned Status: Prospect
Hi {contactfirst}!
This is {name} with web address and Company. I want to thank you again for using one of our websites. Below is a list of properties that match your criteria. I will be contacting you shortly to discuss your needs and better refine your search. If you have any questions in the meantime, please don't hesitate to either email or call me.

To view properties please be sure that your email is set up to accept HTML. You may receive a message "This page contains secure and non-secure items "click here" to unblock content".

Have a great day!
{staffsignature}
{initialPropList}
"You are receiving this email as you either subscribed to one of our websites at or were added by one of our Agents."

Nightly Listings – Homescout
Email Subject Line: Current Listings in County
Initial Drip: 24 Hours & Recurring every 24

Hours

Group Assignment: Search MLS (and any other group you'd like)

Assigned Status: Contact, Prospect, No Drips – Listings Yes

Hi {contactfirst}!

Here is the most recent list of homes that match your criteria. Let me know if you need me to make any changes or if you have any questions about any of these homes. Remember, I can show you any listing in **County**.

Have a great day!

{staffsignature}

"You are receiving this email as you either subscribed to one of our websites at or were added by one of our Agents."

{homeScoutPropList}

Q & A

Email Subject Line: Questions and Answer about your Realtor

Initial Drip: 3 Days

Group Assignment: Search MLS (and any other group you'd like)

Assigned Status:, Prospect, No Listings – Drips Yes

Hi {contactfirst}!

Here is a link to our Q&A letter that addresses commonly asked questions about your Realtor. If you have any questions, please don't hesitate to call or email. Thank you and have a great day!

Q&A: Click Here

{staffsignature}
"You are receiving this email as you either subscribed to one of our websites at or were added by one of our Agents."

Just Checking In Letter – 4 Day
Email Subject Line: Company Listings
Initial Drip: 4 Days
Group Assignment: Search MLS (and any other group you'd like)
Assigned Status: Prospect,

Hi {contactfirst}
I just wanted to take a minute and make sure you are getting the listings I have been sending you. Please let me know if the homes you are receiving fit the homes you are interested in seeing. My goal is to make sure you are getting everything you need to help you make the right choice. If you have any questions as we move through your research stage, please don't hesitate to call or email me. I'm here to help guide you through the process to ensure a smooth and painless home buying experience. Keep in mind I have access to every listing in **County** and can show you any home when needed.

I look forward to helping you. Have a fun day!
{staffsignature}
"You are receiving this email as you either subscribed to one of our websites at or were added by one of our Agents."

Just Checking in Letter – 1 Year Plus
Email Subject Line: Just Checking in with you!

<u>Initial Drip: 21 Days; Recurring 45 Days</u>
<u>Group Assignment: One Year Plus</u>
<u>Assigned Status: Prospect</u>
Hi {contactfirst}
Dear {contactfirst},

I know you are not ready to buy right now, but I did want to make sure the listings I'm sending you match the criteria of the homes you are interested in seeing when you're ready. My goal is to make sure you are getting everything you need to help you make the right choice.

If you have any questions as we move through your research stage, please don't hesitate to call or email me. I'm here to help guide you through the process to ensure a smooth and painless home buying experience. Keep in mind I have access to every listing in **County** and can show you any home when needed.

I look forward to helping you. Have a fun day!

{staffsignature}
"You are receiving this email as you either subscribed to one of our websites at or were added by one of our Agents."

62 Things Your Realtor Does For Buyers

Email Subject Line: Do you know what your Realtor does for you?
<u>Initial Drip: 7 Days</u>
<u>Group Assignment: Search MLS (and any other group you'd like)</u>
<u>Assigned Status: Contact Prospect, No Listings – Drips Yes</u>
Hi {contactfirst}!

Have you ever wondered exactly what your Realtor does for you besides just show you homes? Please click the link below to see my list of duties to help you find your home!

List of things a Realtor does for the buyer: <u>Click Here</u>
{staffsignature}
"You are receiving this email as you either subscribed to one of our websites at or were added by one of our Agents."

<u>School Guide, Tidbits, Brevard Directory</u>
Email Subject Line: Things to Know About County from Company
<u>Initial Drip: 14 Days; Recurring 6 Months</u>
<u>Group Assignment: Search MLS (and any other group you'd like)</u>
<u>Assigned Status: Prospect, No Listings – Drips Yes</u>

Hi {contactfirst}!
There are many contact details you will require when moving to a new area. I have attached some useful links to provide you with everything from utilities to theatres, an A-Z of government organizations and also an education booklet. These are easily accessible by clicking the links and can be printed out for your convenience. I hope this proves useful to you.

Tidbits Guide: <u>Click Here</u>
County Directory: <u>Click Here</u>
Education Booklet: <u>Click Here</u>
Don't hesitate to let me know if there is any further information I can provide you with to make your transition to the area smoother.

{staffsignature}

"You are receiving this email as you either subscribed to one of our websites at or were added by one of our Agents."

Just Checking In Letter – Every 6 Weeks

Email Subject Line: Just Checking In from Company!

Initial Drip: 21 Days; Recurring every 45 days

Group Assignment: Search MLS (and any other group you'd like)

Assigned Status: Prospect, No Listings – Drips Yes

Hi {contactfirst}!

How are you doing? I just wanted to check in to make sure you are receiving all our listing updates. Don't hesitate to email or call me should you have any questions at all. Remember, I can show you any property in **County**!

I look forward to helping you!

{staffsignature}

"You are receiving this email as you either subscribed to one of our websites at or were added by one of our Agents."

Newsletter

(Updated Monthly)

Email Subject Line: Real Estate Newsletter and More!

Initial Drip: 33 Days, Recurring 1 Month
Group Assignment: Search MLS (and any other group you'd like)
Assigned Status: Sold, Contact, Prospect, No Listings – Drips Yes
Hi {contactfirst}!
Check this month's Real Estate Newsletter, which is full of interesting and useful information that I think you will enjoy whether you are a buyer, seller, homeowner or renter.

Newsletter:
http://melbournehomesearch.com/index.cfm/Newsletter

Tropical Realty Tidbits
http://filevault1.colony1.net/10476/UsefulTidbitsGuide.Pdf
Brevard County Customer Service Directory:
http://filevault1.colony1.net/10476/BrevardDirectory.pdf
I have already set you up to receive listings specific to your own criteria; however, for your interest here are Company's In-House listings:

Single Family Homes:
Condo Listings:
Residential Lots and Lands:
If there is anything I can do to refine or update your property criteria, please don't hesitate to call or email me.

{staffsignature}

"You are receiving this email as you either subscribed to one of our websites at or were added by one of our Agents."

No or Bad Phone Number – Initial List Follow Up

Email Subject Line: Follow up on your Property Listings

Initial Drip: 1 Day

Group Assignment: No or Bad Phone Number

Assigned Status: Prospect

Dear {contactfirst}

I would like the opportunity to discuss with you the list of properties I sent you yesterday to ensure I'm sending you the correct properties. Please drop me a note with your phone number and the best time to contact you. If you prefer, we can continue our communication by email, but in the case that these homes do not fit your criteria please drop me a note.

{staffsignature}

"You are receiving this email as you either subscribed to one of our websites at or were added by one of our Agents."

No or Bad Phone Number – Two Week Follow Up

Email Subject Line: Listing Updates - Just Checking In!

Initial Drip: 2 Weeks

Group Assignment: No or Bad Phone Number

Assigned Status: Prospect

Hi {contactfirst}!

Just checking in to make sure you are receiving my updates. If at any time you would like to chat about your home search, please feel free to respond to me with your phone number and the best time to call.

I look forward to helping you!

{staffsignature}

"You are receiving this email as you either subscribed to one of our websites at or were added by one of our Agents."

No or Bad Phone Number – Six Week Follow Up

Email Subject Line: Real Estate Search - How Can I Help you Further?

Initial Drip: 6 Weeks

Group Assignment: No or Bad Phone Number

Assigned Status: Prospect

Hi {contactfirst}!

It's been six weeks since we started your Real Estate Search. In an effort to do the best job I can do for you, I would welcome the opportunity to have a phone discussion. If you are comfortable with that at this point, please respond to this email with your phone number and the best time to call. If you would prefer, please give me a call at anytime.

I look forward to helping you!

{staffsignature}

"You are receiving this email as you either subscribed to one of our websites at or were added by one of our Agents."

No or Bad Phone Number – Ten Week Follow Up

Email Subject Line: Your Real Estate Property Search

Initial Drip: 10 Weeks

Group Assignment: No or Bad Phone Number

Assigned Status: Prospect

Hi {contactfirst}!

I just wanted to take a moment to make sure you are receiving everything I am sending you. If for some reason, this doesn't match your desires, please let me know so I can make the appropriate changes. If you have a moment, I would like to make contact by phone to ensure I am doing everything I can do to help you toward your goal of home ownership. Please send along your phone number if you would like to chat!

I look forward to helping you!

{staffsignature}

"You are receiving this email as you either subscribed to one of our websites at or were added by one of our Agents."

Foreclosure Property

Email Subject Line: Thank you for using web address.

Initial Drip: 30 min

Group Assignment: Foreclosure Property

Assigned Status: Prospect

Hi {contactfirst}!

Thank you for taking the time to use our website at web address.

My name is {name} and I will be contacting you shortly to discuss your Real Estate needs as well as to send you a list of foreclosure properties fitting your criteria. If you have any questions in the meantime, feel free to contact me at {phone1} or Email {email1}.

I have added your name to our update system, which will notify you of any new foreclosure listings and/or changes in listings fitting your criteria. The notification will have LISTINGS CART UPDATE or CURRENT LISTINGS IN COUNTY in the subject line. The Listing Updates will be coming from either {name} at innovia@brevardmls.com or {email1} and may be sent to your spam folder. Please remember to check your spam folder.

If you have any Real Estate questions, or would like to view any listings, please don't hesitate to contact me at {phone1}. I can show you ANY property listing in COUNTY!

Again, thank you and I look forward to helping you!

Have a great day!
{staffsignature}
"You are receiving this email as you either subscribed to one of our websites at or were added by one of our Agents."

Listing Updates

Email Subject Line: Listing Updates from web address

Initial Drip: 30 Min
Group Assignment: Listing Updates
Assigned Status: Prospect
Hi {contactfirst}!
Thank you for taking the time to use our website at web address.

My name is {name} and I will be contacting you shortly to discuss your Real Estate needs as well as to send you a list of homes fitting your criteria. If you have any questions in the meantime, feel free to contact me at {phone1} or Email {email1}.

I have added your name to our update system, which will notify you of any new listings and/or changes in listings fitting your criteria. The notification will have LISTING UPDATES in the subject line. The Listing Updates will be coming from {email1} and may be sent to your spam folder. Please remember to check your spam folder.

If you have any Real Estate questions, or would like to view any listings, please don't hesitate to contact me at {phone1}. I can show you ANY property listing in County!

Again, thank you and I look forward to helping you!

Have a great day!

{staffsignature}

"You are receiving this email as you either subscribed to one of our websites at or were added by one of our Agents."

Market Analysis

Email Subject Line: Market Analysis from Company

Initial Drip: 30 Min

Group Assignment: Market Analysis

Assigned Status: Prospect

Hi {contactfirst}!

Thank you for taking the time to request a Market Analysis on our website, web address.

My name is {name} and I will be contacting you shortly to discuss your Real Estate needs as well as to prepare your Market Analysis. If you have any questions in the meantime, feel free to contact me at {phone1} or Email {email1}.

Again, thank you and I look forward to helping you!

Have a great day!

{staffsignature}

"You are receiving this email as you either subscribed to one of our websites at or were added by one of our Agents."

Relocation Packet

Email Subject Line: Thank you for requesting a Relocation Packet!

<u>Initial Drip: 30 Minutes</u>

<u>Group Assignment: Relocation Packet</u>

<u>Assigned Status: Prospect and Contact</u>

Hi {contactfirst}!

Thank you for requesting a Relocation Packet and taking the time to visit web address.

My name is {name} and I will be sending you a Relocation Packet. If you have any questions in the meantime, feel free to contact me at {phone1} or Email {email1}.

If you would like to view any listings, please don't hesitate to contact me at {phone1}. I can show you ANY property listing in County!

Again, thank you and I look forward to helping you!

Have a great day!

{staffsignature}

"You are receiving this email as you either subscribed to one of our websites at or were added by one of our Agents."

Ask the Realtor

Email Subject Line: Thank you for using web address.

Initial Drip: 30 Min
Group Assignment: Ask the Realtor
Assigned Status: Prospect

Hi {contactfirst}!

Thank you for taking the time to use our website at web address.

My name is {name} and I will be contacting you shortly to discuss the question that you've submitted. If you need anything in the meantime, feel free to contact me at {phone1} or Email {email1}.

If you have any other Real Estate questions, or would like to view any listings, please don't hesitate to contact me at {phone1}. I can show you ANY property listing in County!

Again, thank you and I look forward to helping you!

Have a great day!

{staffsignature}

"You are receiving this email as you either subscribed to one of our websites at or were added by one of our Agents."

First Sold Contact

Email Subject Line: Congratulations!
Initial Drip: 1 Day
Group Assignment: Sold

Assigned Status: Sold
Hi {contactfirst}!

Congratulations! Thanks for all your cooperation and patience throughout the entire transaction! Let me know if there is anything I can do for you.
{staffsignature}
"You are receiving this email as you either subscribed to one of our websites at or were added by one of our Agents."

2 Weeks Sold
Email Subject Line: How Are You?
Initial Drip: 2 Weeks
Group Assignment: Sold
Assigned Status: Sold
Hi {contactfirst}!

I just wanted to check in and make sure everything is going okay with the property and to see whether or not you need help in any way.
If there's anything you need please email me or give me a call!

{staffsignature}
"You are receiving this email as you either subscribed to one of our websites at or were added by one of our Agents."

30 Days Sold
Email Subject Line: Make sure to file for a Homestead exemption
Initial Drip: 30 Days

Group Assignment: Sold
Assigned Status: Sold
Hi {contactfirst}!

How is everything going? Here is the County Tax Appraiser's office site should you need information to file your homestead exemption.

Tax Appraisers website

{staffsignature}
"You are receiving this email as you either subscribed to one of our websites at or were added by one of our Agents."

3 Months Sold
Email Subject Line: Just Checking in With You
Initial Drip: 3 Months
Group Assignment: Sold
Assigned Status: Sold
Hi {contactfirst}!

I just wanted to check in with you and see how you are doing? I hope you've had the chance to check out some of the great restaurants that County has to offer. If you haven't visited the website for dining, entertainment and shopping, just click the link below:

http://www.dining-out-guide.com/

{staffsignature}
"You are receiving this email as you either subscribed to one of our websites at or were added by

one of our Agents."

6 Months Sold
Email Subject Line: Just Thinking about You
Initial Drip: 6 Months
Group Assignment: Sold
Assigned Status: Sold
Hi {contactfirst}!

I just wanted you to know I'd been thinking about you and hope everything is going well. If there is anything I can do for you in the future or should you have any friends, family or neighbors who need the help of a Realtor, please keep me in mind.

{staffsignature}
"You are receiving this email as you either subscribed to one of our websites at or were added by one of our Agents."

One Year Sold
Email Subject Line: Congratulations to you and your home!
Initial Drip: 1 Year
Group Assignment: Sold
Assigned Status: sold
Hi {contactfirst}!
Happy Anniversary! Can you believe it's been a year since you purchased your home?
{staffsignature}
"You are receiving this email as you either subscribed to one of our websites at or were added by one of our Agents."

1.5 Years Sold

Email Subject Line: I Can't Believe it's Been a Year and A Half!

Initial Drip: 18 Months
Group Assignment: Sold
Assigned Status: Sold

Hi {contactfirst}!

I just wanted to let you know that I've been thinking about you and hope everything is going really well. I can't believe it's already been a year and a half since you bought your property. Keep in touch and let me know how things are going with you.

Should any of your friends, family or neighbors require the services of a Realtor in the future, please keep me in mind.

{name}, Realtor
Tropical Realty of Suntree, Inc. of Suntree, Inc
{phone1}
{email1}
www.mitchrealty.com
www.melbournehomesearch.com

"You are receiving this email as you either subscribed to one of our websites at or were added by one of our Agents."

2.5 Years Sold

Email Subject Line: Sometimes you need work done on your home

Initial Drip: 30 Months

<u>Group Assignment: Sold</u>
<u>Assigned Status: Sold</u>
Hi {contactfirst}!

I know sometimes you need work done at your house on things like AC, Roof, Electrical and more. If you need any help finding good people to do this, please let me know and I will gladly send them your way!

{staffsignature}
"You are receiving this email as you either subscribed to one of our websites at or were added by one of our Agents."

3 Years Sold

Email Subject Line: It's Been 3 Years Since You Bought Your Home!

<u>Initial Drip: 36 Months</u>
<u>Group Assignment: Sold</u>
<u>Assigned Status: Sold</u>
Hi {contactfirst}!

Where does the time go? It's been three years and you are still in the same house! Actually, it's now a home after all this time.

{staffsignature}
"You are receiving this email as you either subscribed to one of our websites at or were added by one of our Agents."

Chapter Forty-Two: Drip Campaigns

I am asked on a daily basis to explain the difference between Agents who are successful with Internet Leads verses those who are not successful. The answer is quite simple…phone calls. Over the years I have seen many Agents who don't want to make calls. There isn't one of them that were successful with Internet Leads. In fact, only a couple of them have been successful in Real Estate.

If you read any sales book on the market, they all have one thing in common, it's prospecting. The beauty of a lead system is that it is not cold calling. It's warm calling. Think of this, use yourself as an example, when you register on an Internet Site, do you supply a correct phone number if you don't want them to call you? Of course you don't. However if you want them to call you, you do. I have asked hundreds of people this question and I have yet to have anyone tell me they would give a good phone number. Therefore, it's safe to say that since the leads gave you a good phone number, they are expecting a call. The number one response we receive from our calls is, "Thank you so much for calling. We've registered on many sites and you are the first person to ever call." Make your calls!

So why are making calls so important? There are only 4 aspects that are consistent with almost every business; Capturing Leads, Nurturing Leads, Closing Leads and then Follow Up after the sale to create a customer for life. The entire process isn't always about setting an appointment, although that is the goal. It's about building relationships. Real Estate is a relationship built business. It's all about building long lasting relationships. The goal of the phone call is to help build those relationships.

Making a connection on the phone is as important or almost as important as discussing their Real Estate needs. Yes, talking about Real Estate is important and finding out their needs along with their buying timeframe are huge. However, understanding their personal life is just as important to build the bond that will help building trust and loyalty. Spend more of your time discussing their family and their lifestyle. Show an honest interest in finding out more about the lead verses their being just a possible transaction. Remember, it's about creating a relationship. Most of your leads will not buy a home today. They might buy in a month, three months, a year or more. This past year over 80 sales came from leads that were more than 3 years old. You heard that right. Why were we able to convert that many "old" leads? Phone calls!

Below are the key points you should hit on while making your first call. Subsequent calls need to be based on the content and results of the first phone call.

• Buying Timeframe – After some small talk, one of the most important pieces of information you need to find out is when they are buying. Your entire follow up process and time table relies on this answer.

• Children or Retiring – What stage of life are they going to be in when they make the move? If they have children, are they school aged children. You will need to find out what they want in a school. Maybe they have children but want to be near the beach. Again, good schools beachside. If they are retiring, what are they looking to do for fun during their retirement? Are they going to boat? Then looking at canal or waterfront properties might be the answer. Do they want to live in a 55+ community? Do they want to live near a golf course?

- Lifestyle – What do they like to do for fun? Do they travel a lot? Then maybe a condo might work best. Do they need to be near the airport? We have two within close proximity to our county. Do they boat, golf, play tennis or something else? We offer a tremendous amount of lifestyle activities. The more you know about what they do outside of their job, the better chance you have of building a relationship.

- First time homebuyer – If so, it's important that they understand all aspects of buying a home, especially financing. If they are buying within the next few months, it's important that they talk to a lender to discuss their options, but mostly to understand how much home they will qualify for.

- Real Estate – Of course finding out their exact needs to buying a home is critical for them to continue to use your site. This involves listening to them as they discuss the type of home they are interested in purchasing. If you are sending info that isn't relative to their needs, then they will move on to another site and another Realtor.

- Pre – Qualification – If they are buying within the next few months, it's important to find out if they will need financing. It's always best to get your customer pre-approved before they come to the area. As with first time Homebuyers, not only is it important to find out if they can obtain financing, but also what home price they can afford. Keep in mind that there will be many Buyers (about 30%) that are going to be paying cash. Also keep in mind that many people will not be comfortable giving you or anyone they don't know financial information over the phone. Be patient and understanding. I am always willing to give any potential customer 4 hours of my time showing homes. After my initial 4 hours, if they are serious about buying, they will need to talk to a lender.

In the end, your phone call relationship is going to make or break your career if you are a lead driven Realtor. Internet Leads are the now and future of Real Estate, yet the phone call and future follow up is more important than the lead you capture. Without proper follow up and relationship building, you will lose about 75% of the business you could have earned. There are no short cuts. Be patient. Don't be in a hurry to get off the phone. This isn't a race about how many conversations you can have, but how many relationships you can cultivate. It's not rocket science. It's planned success. You can do it if you put your mind and your work ethic into it.

Chapter Forty-Three: Listing Objections, Buyer Objections

The other Agent will take less for the listing, why won't you?

I can understand your desire to save a few dollars, but my commission is 6%. If an Agent will immediately discount their commission, how would they do during the negotiation of your home? We are worth every bit of what we charge.

Assist to sell will only charge me $750 to sell my home why should I list with you?

I have heard this before. I also have heard that they took money and didn't sell the home. We only get paid if we sell your home. In reality, if they are only making $750 on your house, and they get their money upfront, how motivated to you think they are to sell your house? In fact, the longer your house is on the market, the better for them. (their model is to list a home and get at least 5 buyer leads from it)

My house is better than the house that just sold down the street and it sold for more than you say my house is worth.

I understand your thoughts, but the market has changed and we have to use current comps to determine the pricing of your home. If we don't price your home appropriately it will not sell. As you can see by the comps I used, these homes all sold in the last 3 months and they determine the value of

your home.

My house has a $60k pool. Why isn't my house worth $60k more than the same house down the street?

Unfortunately, items such as pool prices don't translate to an equal value in home prices. A pool certainly adds some value, but it's closer to $5k- $10k.

I need to get this much for my house or I can't move

I understand that one! However, the reality is I don't set the home prices, the Buyers and the market determine the home prices. As you can see by the comps, similar homes have sold at this price. You told me that you have to move for a new job in 90 days. What happens if you don't sell your home?

I bought a house 3 years ago and the Agent told me that it would be worth more when I sold it. Why is your sales price so low?

I wish we all had crystal balls. The reality is, we don't determine the market. I determine prices strictly on the numbers. They don't lie. Based on the comps in this area, this IS the price your home should sell at.

I have multiple people involved in this transaction and they cannot all be here.

Let's discuss how we can deal with this. Are you able to get a power of attorney for the other folks involved? How do you plan on handling the transaction or approval of any offers?

My home is not a short sale or foreclosure so I don't want to sell it at that price.

Unfortunately, market values are driven by short sales and foreclosures. There have been 5 sales

in this area and all have been short sales. Appraisers, by law, have to use short sales and foreclosures to determine market values. That is the reality of our current market.

Zillow says my house is worth much more than you are telling me.

We hear this all the time. Unfortunately Zillow is a marketing site with data that does not take local market conditions into affect. Based on the comps that I have found of properties that sold in your neighborhood, this price is the right price to sell.

I don't want to lower my sales price.

Nobody wants to lower their price. The reality is, we can keep the house priced where it is, but it's been on the market for 6 months without any showings. It's all about exposure and price. We have the exposure, but with no showings it's about price. The comps don't lie. As I told you when I listed the home with you, it's not worth $500,000, it's worth $400,000. Until we get within range of the actual price, it won't sell.

My home is better than the home down the street. It should be worth more.

In this market it's all about price and exposure. If you look at the last three homes that have sold in this neighborhood, these are the prices that determine your value. The home down the street sold 2 years ago at that price. A lot has changed since then. These current homes on the market have been on for (x amount of days) at this price. If you really want to sell your home, this price will have to be (x)

I only want to list my house with a big name company.

I hear that a lot. Keep in mind just because a company has a national name doesn't mean they can sell your home any quicker. The reality is a person is going to buy your home if it is priced right. We all do very similar marketing, from listing it in the MLS to showcasing it on our websites. And, because of our extensive marketing, your home will show up on all Realtor websites in the area. Bigger is not always better!

I paid $250,000 and can't sell for less than I paid.

Unfortunately, you are not alone. Anyone that bought a home from 2004-2006 is not going to get what they paid for it. Let's look at your options if you can't sell it for (x) price. You can either stay in the house and hope for values to go back up in the next couple years or you can move and rent the property. We can't control the pricing, it is what it is.

I think I will try to sell my home on my own for a while.

I think that's a great idea. The key of course is to make sure you price your house correctly, disclose all that's wrong with the house, be available to show your home when the buyer wants to look and purchase the correct advertising for your home. There is a reason why 90% of all For Sale By Owner homes end up being sold by a Realtor.

I was told that I should interview 3 Agents before deciding which Realtor to use. Why should I choose you before interviewing the others?

That's simple. You won't find an Agent that is going to tell you like it is and who will work harder to sell your home. With that said, selling your home is about price and exposure. We not only expose your home to more Buyers than anyone else in the area through our Internet marketing, but we also market your home on almost every Agent website and to every Agent in the county. So yes, you can spend your time interviewing 3 Agents, listening to 3 sales pitches and then trying to decipher between what is real and what is not or you can just hire me. Would you like to get started with the paperwork?

How many customers will you bring to see my home?

That's impossible for me to tell you right now. No Agent could tell you. In reality, because of our extensive marketing, many people that we hit are already working with another Realtor. These people dictate to their Agents which homes they want to see. You will get more showings on your home, whether we bring them in the door or our marketing brings them in through other Agents. It doesn't matter. It's about selling your home right?

Charlie with Brand X has a TV show. How come you don't?

We spend our marketing on proven results. We have tested so many marketing programs and the reality is that nothing even comes close to the results we see from our Internet marketing.

I'm not going to give my house away.

I don't want you to give your house away. I want you to get as much money for it as possible.

With that said, this is the price of your home based on today's market. Maybe you shouldn't be selling your home right now.

Buyer Objections

I am worried about what is going to happen when the Space Center closes. (this could be any adverse issue applicable to your county or area)

It's a worry for everyone. However, the reality is, we have been at the bottom of the market for quite some time now and homes priced correctly are selling quickly. Interest rates are the lowest they have been in years and will be going up. Each point the interest rates go up, the more you pay for your home, even if the price is a little lower. There is always something going on in the area or the world that can affect home prices.

I am going to wait until the bottom of the market.

We have been level now since January 2010, which is where the market actually hit bottom. We *are* at the bottom. As of this book's publication it is the perfect time to buy with prices at their lowest in 10 years and interest rates at a 50 year low. Your ability to buy will change dramatically when interest rates rise, which they will.

I'm not going to commit to you because I feel I need more than one Agent working for me so I get the best house.

I have heard that many times. The reality is no Agent will work in your best interest when you are using multiple Agents. They know they have one shot to SELL you a house. When you work with one Agent, me, I work in your best interest to help you

find your home.

I will not get a preapproval letter until I find the right house.

If we find a home you love, we have to have a preapproval letter to submit an offer. In this market, even people with great credit have been turned down for financing. I would hate for you to find the home of your dreams only to find out you don't qualify for a mortgage of that amount.

I don't want to live in a (protected class) area but I want the 5 bedroom house with a pool under $100k.

As you can see, this is the list of homes in the area you want that are 5 bedrooms with a pool. There are none in the price range you are looking to spend. Your options are to either pick a different area or change your criteria on the home you are looking to buy.

I'm worried about crime in the area and the amount of absentee owners.

Crime is everywhere. I would suggest contacting the police and asking them about any area you are interested in buying to see how the area has been.

I'm unsure of which school district will work best for me.

Here is the website to check out the ratings of the schools. This will help you decide which area you want to raise your children.

I need to sell a home first

Is it listed yet? If so, then is it priced correctly? How long has it been on the market? Do you have your Realtor's phone number so I can see

how it is going? I can show you a few homes so you can get an idea of what you can get for your money, but the reality is, the homes currently on the market will most likely not be on the market once your home is under contract. We are better off looking at different areas and deciding which area we should concentrate our search on for when you do sell your home.

I have heard bad things about Palm Bay, but like the prices (This could be anywhere with lower pricing)

Palm Bay, like most areas has it's issues, but we have sold a bunch of homes there and I haven't heard of any problems. Palm Bay has some of the best homes for the money in the county. However, we can always look in a different area if that makes you more comfortable, let me send you a list of homes with your criteria throughout the county so you can see what you can get for your money.

I'm waiting for the right home.

Tell me everything you need in a home for it to be the perfect home. Let's find that for you today!

I have to see what I get out of the sale of my house before I can buy.

Great, I can appreciate that. I will gladly do a net sheet for you to figure out roughly what you will get based on market values. As we know, the numbers are the numbers. Once you know roughly what you will receive, then we can determine what you can buy.

It's a Buyer's market. I should be able to get this home much cheaper.

Yes, it sure is a Buyer's market which has driven the prices down over 50% since 2005. The

reality is, this home is priced right where it should be and homes priced correctly are selling at 92.8% of their listing price.

I'm just looking at the area and deciding if we want to move there.

I can appreciate that. What we should do then is schedule a few hours to drive to different areas in the county. Once you decide you like the area, we can then look at a variety of homes in the areas of the county you would like to live.

I won't be ready to buy for a year, but will be in the area and want to take a look.

I can appreciate that. What we should do then is schedule a few hours to drive to different areas in the county. Once you decide you like the area, we can then look at a variety of homes in the areas of the count you would like to live.

I want to wait to speak to a lender and have my credit checked.

I understand that, but homes that are priced correctly are selling quickly. Without being preapproved, you won't know exactly what price you qualify to buy. There is nothing worse than finding the home of your dreams and not qualifying for that home. Things are much different in the lending world today than they were a few years ago.

What will this home be worth next year?

Don't we all wish we had a crystal ball? It's impossible to know for sure. None of us expected the crash to be quite as hard as it was. The reality is, you are buying this home as a home. Prices can go up or down, but if you don't plan on moving in the next 7 years, then the price isn't as relative.

I had heard that I can buy a house in (your city) for about half price.

You are right! Houses have fallen around 50% since 2005. Right now houses are selling at 92.8% of their asking prices which means that the homes on the market, listed correctly, are at market value and will sell close to, if not more than, their list price.

I'm only planning on offering really low offers until I find an owner that will accept one.

I can understand that. Everyone is looking for a deal right now. The reality is, homes are selling close to their asking price and anything that IS a deal is selling very quickly and with multiple offers.

(Follow-up & Reply) That's fine, but that is what I plan on doing.

Again, I understand. However, you are not going to find a $1,000,000 house for $500,000. I wouldn't be able to help you if you were not realistic in home values.

I want to make low ball offers on all 5 homes that we looked at and then decide which home I really want to buy when I get their bottom dollars.

Not a problem. We legally have to disclose this to the other Agent when writing these offers or you could easily receive multiple signed contracts. You will then have expenses trying to get out of those contracts. Are you okay with having to do home inspections on properties you are not going to buy?

I will probably have to pay cash to buy a home and won't need a bank.

That's great. Then what I need for your file is

your proof of funds. Any offer we make is going to need a copy of your proof of funds to submit the offer. Do you want to use my computer to pull up your bank account?

I want to look at 30 homes this weekend.

One of the reasons you use a Realtor is so you don't have to look at 30 homes in a weekend. Once you get past 5 or 6 in a day they all run together. I have looked at the 30 homes you requested and pulled the best 5 in the bunch. These homes are far superior than the other homes you wanted to look at. My job is to find you your dream home. Believe me, after looking at 30 homes you will be very confused. That's my job to find the best of the best for you!

Chapter Forty-Four: Be the Boss

What can you do to make the changes you need to make to increase your business?

First, we need to look at what is causing you to not obtain your goals. It's usually not what you are doing; it's what you are not doing that really impacts your results. Obviously, you have obtained some success in your career. However, are you reaching your goals? Why not? Usually it's a lack of structure in your personal life and business life that adversely affects you the most.

Structure

This is the killer of most Agents. You are an independent contractor which means you have no boss, per say. This was your dream wasn't it? You are completely in control of your life and your future.

However, you most likely never owned your own business in the past and this is a problem. Do you have the self-motivation to keep building your business? Are you finding that you wake up in the morning and take a little longer to get out of bed? Breakfast lasts until 10am now and lunch starts at 11:30am. Ahhh structure. Of course this type of structure is why 99% of all Realtors fail in their first year!

Here is the problem. If you are not willing to do the work, who is going to do it for you? You have two choices, the way I see it: get to work or get a regular job where you are doing whatever the boss tells you to do. Of course you will now be back in the grind that you chose to leave. And you are putting a cap on your income opportunities. Let's face it, as a Realtor, for very little investment, you can earn as much as you desire....as long as you are willing to work for it. Second, you could become more disciplined in your work life as a Realtor. Can you do this? Of course you can! Will you do this? I don't know!

So let's look at your first assignment to start your move toward the next level of you productivity.

Before you can fix the problem, you need to understand the problem. To me, Time Management and Structure are your two biggest enemies...and yourself, of course! Over the next 7 days, I want you to take a piece of paper and track everything you do. This means from the time you wake up each morning to the end of the day when you go to bed. Our goal with this exercise is to find out how you are really spending your days, not how you think you are spending your days. There is always a big difference!

Once you get a handle on how you are really spending your days, you can spend time fixing this. However, none of this means anything if you don't make the commitment to yourself to make these changes. I can't make you do anything, and I certainly can't do the work for you. But you have it in you to make these changes. You can continue to blame the market or whatever story you have told yourself, but the reality is, and I've said this before, the only person holding you back is you.

So what do you need to do to start adding structure to your life? To me, the first thing that has helped to accomplish as much as I accomplish is to write out my list of what needs to be done every morning.

It's usually the first thing I do in the morning and the last thing I look at when I go home at night. Every morning when I get to the office, I spend the first 15 minutes planning my day. I may write down 10 things, but the reality is I'm only going to accomplish 6 of these things so I take the 6 most important activities that must get done today. I always try to accomplish the hardest of these tasks first thing in the morning as it becomes more difficult as the day goes on.

I can hear you all mumbling from here. I know you are all saying that I spend my day reacting to my customer's needs. I can never plan my day because my customers control my time. Hmmm. Does that mean something or what? Your customers control your time. We will get back to that one in a bit! Here you are again, making excuses why you can't be more organized and you can't be successful. Why do you keep doing this? Why are you always trying to talk yourself out of being successful? I personally don't understand it, yet I see it every day from Agents in my office to friends of mine who are always telling me how they are going to do this and that, yet never do. Am I yelling at you? No! You should be yelling at yourself. If you choose to continue down the path you are most likely going, that choice is your choice. I'm simply pointing out what I observe on a daily basis with Agents all around the country.

Okay, time for a story. I spent a couple weeks ago helping a team of Agents get a better handle on their lead conversion issues. They have been members of the Network for some time now, but they have not really been following my systems. They listen to all my stuff and read all my material and then go on doing business the way they have been doing it for years...and just doing okay. They all want to get to the next level as I'm sure you all do too, but are they willing to get out of their own way.

It turns out, after spending the first afternoon with the team leader, that he is spending all of his time trying to perfect his website and his IDX and so on and so on. He is doing everything he can to avoid actually going after new business. They have over 3,000 leads in their system and are not really converting many of them. It dawned on me after I left that he is using the website stuff as a way to, in his mind, justify why he can't be successful in his business. It's the website's fault, not his. To be a good leader, you must first lead by example. I'm a huge believer in proving everything I do before I teach to either you or my Agents. For this guy to really get his team to take the next step in growing their business, then he is going to have to stop hiding behind the website issues and go out and sell some homes.

With all that said, I got an email yesterday that the team has been working their database and organizing their leads. From making phone calls the past week they have two $1 million dollar Buyers and two $3 million Buyers that they have rejuvenated. I would say that's some mighty fine results! Did I really say that?

Okay, so let's get back to structuring your day. Your goal should be, as much as possible, to turn your business into a proactive business verse a reactive business. I understand that sometimes things come up that we need to deal with at that moment. That is part of our business. However, if you really are going to become successful, which means selling at least 50+ homes per year, then you are going to have to change your mindset on how you run your business. Structure will help you do this. Another quick story.

In 2004 I got married to my awesome wife, Jeanette. We were married March 20th and had a great wedding. I even put my old band back together and sang the wedding song I wrote for my wife. On top of that, a friend of mine is the singer for the band Orleans (Still the One and Dance with Me). He came and played on my song while we played those two hits for our 180 guests. It was awesome. My stepdaughter was also getting married in July of that year. As you can imagine, paying for two fairly large weddings was pretty daunting and I had to make over $100k to pay for two weddings and of course my taxes. I worked my tail off from January through July 31st of that year. I paid my taxes, which were ridiculous, and I paid for both weddings. I was pretty proud. Unfortunately though, I had only taken 5 days off including both weddings. On July 31st I was floating down the Ichetucknee Springs in North West Florida. It was a beautiful day with my wife, stepson, Michael, and his girlfriend, Melanie. After floating in the spring for two hours, I became ill. I wasn't sure what was going on. I told my wife that something bad was happening, but knowing that I joke about everything, she thought I was fooling. My eyes then rolled back in my head and I went over into the water. My wife still thought I was fooling until she realized that there was no way I was going into 50 degree water. Heck, I only go in my pool when it hits 85 or 90 degrees!

I was underwater for 10 seconds before I came up to see my wife swimming toward me and some guy grabbing me by the neck to get me on board his inner tube. Luckily, we were only 100 yards from the end of the spring. They got me back to shore and called the ambulance. I went out again before they got there. Once there, the paramedics could not get a blood pressure reading. I went out again. Obviously, something was very wrong! I was scared, my wife was scared and the kids were scared…it was very scary! Before I knew it, I was in an ambulance getting a needle in my arm and on the way to the hospital. But it gets worse! Because they couldn't get a blood pressure, they felt they needed to give me an epi. This is normally 3/10ths of a cc but they gave me 3 cc's! Now, on top of what was going on, I went into convulsions and thought I was going to die. By the look of the EMT, he probably thought the same thing! They finally got me to the hospital and got my heart settled down and determined that I went into anaphylaxis shock from an allergic reaction. So between the heart almost bursting and the allergic reaction, I was as close to dying than I would ever want to be again! So what's the point of this story?

That was the point in my life that I changed my life, my attitude and stopped being reactive and became proactive! It was a huge turning point as I knew how close I was to losing my life. There wasn't one second while I thought I was dying that I thought about work or anything to do with work. I was thinking about my wife and kids. That was it. Everything else was unimportant. I realized that no matter how hard I worked, if I didn't take some time to enjoy the fruits of my labor, there was no sense to it all. Being proactive changes everything. You become the professional instead of the punching bag. From that day forward, I spend Sundays with my wife. Sunday is her day and even if it means me sitting in a store while she shops for shoes, I do it.

Of course, by making this decision I assumed I would lose customers. After all, by this time, almost all my business was coming from online. I had built loyalty with many of my leads, but how loyal would they be? A funny thing happened. I didn't lose any customers when I told them I didn't work on Sundays because that was my family day. But I also told them that if they really needed to see something on a Sunday, I would have one of my coworkers help them out. I can't remember losing one customer to this new found proactivity. Is that a word?

If my customers don't mind me taking the day off with my wife, maybe I was reading more into their thought than was really going on. In other words, maybe I wouldn't be at their whims anymore, I could actually control the experience and actually come off as more professional. It worked! Not only did I not lose customers, but I started feeling like I had a little bit of a life. This gave me some recharge time so I could not only enjoy the day with my wife, but I was also allowed the luxury to rethink some of my business operations. It was the beginning of taking control of my customers.

So what does this have to do with structure? Everything! Unless you are willing to be bold and stick up for your life, then you may never be able to find this sense of control. When you are able to control your life by controlling your customers, you are able to form a more structured business. Each day can be on your terms and not on your customer's terms. As I have said, there are times when you have to relinquish your control to accommodate a customer, but the majority of the time you will be in control, able to start the next step of your new structured business.

Next, we need to talk about your structured day. The biggest mistake I see, and I see it every day in my office and offices I visit all around the country, is Realtors who don't feel the need to build their business. They sit at their desks, read the newspaper and wait to be reactive to whoever calls them. These are the Agents that went from doing 30 transactions in 2004 to 3 transactions in 2009. They have a desire to be successful, but they really don't want to do what it takes. So how do you become successful in any market? Prospecting!

Prospecting is the key to success in any business. I don't care what type of business you have, you have to be able to create leads and then follow up with those leads. As you all know, I have owned a ton of businesses. Most have done well for one reason: I spent the majority of my time building customers.

The reason is obvious. No customers means no revenue, which means no income, which means a whole bunch of bad stuff! Prospecting is the life blood of any business.

The next question out of your mouth is where do you start? This is a great question and it can be different for so many of you. However, the easiest place to start is right in your own backyard. Does everyone you know, know you are a Realtor? Does your Uncle in NY know? Calling your circle of influence and past customers is the easiest form of prospecting. You should make it a point to touch base at least once a quarter. Everyone knows someone who is buying or selling a home. You need to be the first person that comes to their mind when they think Real Estate. Why calling verse email? It's pretty simple, email is impersonal. A two minute phone call is going to go a lot further than a paragraph email.

Sure, email has its place in building business. But it really doesn't do well in building a great personal relationship with your customer. Yes, I know there are many exceptions, but the reality is, a phone call goes much further.

Once you have contacted your circle of influence, the next step is to figure out exactly who you want to call. There are bunches of ways to go about this. You can call expireds, withdrawn and FSBOs. Those are the obvious first ones, and they are also the ones that get called on a regular basis. You can call a specific neighborhood and let them know you are there to help. You can get a list of people who are about to be served with foreclosure notices and help them with their situations. My favorite of course is to build a huge database of Buyers and Sellers and continue to work that base. We do this at our office through our Internet Marketing efforts. With that said, even though we do okay with listings, the majority, huge majority, of our Internet Marketing is toward Buyers. Over the past 4 years we spent our time building our buyer database as it didn't make good business sense to be a listing Agent. We are currently adding listings to our marketing, but I haven't come up with a great online marketing effort that is predictable. It's something I'm working on and getting ready to test. Once I get it figured out, and I will, I will certainly pass it along!

Your database can and will be the lifeblood of your business if you are prescribing to our *100MPH system.* In 2008 we launched our software, *100MPH Marketing and Lead Conversion*, to help us automate the lead conversion process as much as we can. It's currently available in Florida, Washington, DC, parts of Virginia, and parts of Maryland (MRIS). This system does a ton behind the scenes to help convert more leads to sales. Feel free to contact me if you would like a demo or to discuss how the software can help you. In the meantime, you can follow the *100MPH System* manually, which is what we did for the first 7 years after we implemented the program. Our database has grown to almost 40,000 Buyers and it's contains a wealth of business. We now know that almost half of these Buyers are opening our emails. That's an amazing number of people reading our emails. I had honestly thought that maybe 20% or so were reading them, but we actually have 20% of our Buyers logging into our system on a regular basis. So look at those numbers: 20,000 people are reading our emails and 8,000 people are logging in on a regular basis. This is the easiest form of prospecting. You simply pick up the phone, for the ones that have phone numbers, and call to check in. The key to Internet Marketing for Real Estate is taking your leads and building a personal loyalty-based relationship with them. This happens with phone calls. Where most Agents are cold calling to do their prospecting, we have an endless supply of people to call and to find the ones who are going to buy or sell a home soon. Our goal, of course, is to find someone buying in the next 30 days.

One of our Agents, on her first day of calls, talked to a guy who was working with a few Agents. She told him he needed to make a decision and use only one Agent. He chose her and not only put a contract on a home the following week, but he also referred two more customers to her that have put contracts on homes. If she hadn't called this person, she wouldn't have sold three homes!

Once you put structure in your life, so many more opportunities will come to you. You will now be working to increase your business by putting yourself in front of as many people as you want daily.

I recently spent a week at a Mike Ferry Conference. Even though I'm not a cold call type person, I was very struck by all the Realtors I met, all dressed professionally. And the number one common denominator was, they all go to work each day. Do you?

I talked to so many Agents during the week in Vegas and they all answered the question the same way. My question was: what do you contribute your success to in this business? They all answered that they lead very structured lives that include daily prospecting for new business. And they all said they went to work each day. The question is, if you were getting paid $100,000 a year by an employer and they said that you needed to spend Monday through Friday, from 9am – 1pm making phone calls to generate business, would you? Almost every one of you said of course! Then why won't you do that for yourself? Then you will make $100,000 or more! It takes determination and discipline. You need to run your business like a business. You need to get up in the morning, go to the office, dress professionally and spend 80% of your time building your business.

When most Agents are spending 5% or their time or less building their businesses, you will lead the pack almost immediately. I guarantee you that if you spend 80% of your time building your business (and this doesn't mean thinking about building your business) you will be amazed and blessed with so much in return. This is one business where you get everything you give. If you give it all, you can have it all!

Take at least 5 or 6 hours of your day and commit it to a structured life. Do this every day for the next 6 months. Make it your habit. Make it who you are. Is it easy? Of course not. As they say, if it were easy, everyone would do it. There are very few Realtors who actually make money in this business.

How much money you make is directly related to how structured you run your life and your business. If you want to sit by the phone and wait for that great buyer or seller to call you, that's up to you. Me, I would rather control my life and my income. I would prefer to know that I have a plan and a mission that will help guide me through to success. Wake up each day knowing that today is a completely new day and you can accomplish. Everything you want to accomplish, just do it!

Once your business grows and is doing 50+ sales per year, it's a piece of cake to take the next step. You can always grow. I believe the saying is if you are not growing you are dying. I have had a bunch of my friends ask me why I'm always testing new ideas and new concepts to grow my companies. The answer is simple: I always want to be ahead of the game. I always want to figure out simple systems that work to increase my business.

Every year my goal for my company grows. I never rest on my laurels. Sometimes I win, and sometime I lose. It's just a way of life in the business world. The worst thing you can do though is to not try! That is the true sign of failure. I have had two major financial losses in my life. Both were devastating to both my family and me. However, my most memorable learning experiences come from those two losses. I have learned much more losing businesses than I have learned succeeding in business. Don't let yourself down.

Okay, so let's get started right this minute.

1. Write down your goals for the next 12 months. Write down your business goals and your personal goals. Be realistic but also don't be so easy on yourself that you are not challenged.

2. Go look in the mirror once you are done with your goals and make an honest commitment to yourself and your family that you are going to accomplish these goals and make building your business a priority. Solidify the commitment!

3. Look at each of your goals and break them down into quarterly, monthly, weekly and daily activities. Let's look at that for a minute. How do you break your goals down? Let's first consider a few truths within my office:

a. Our close rate in this market is 33%. This means if I want to sell 50 homes this coming 12 months I need to work with 150 people.

b. To do 4 sales per month, I need to work with 12 different people per month.

c. We know that 50% of the people we schedule appointments with will cancel or postpone. This means I need 24 scheduled appointments to receive 12 shows.

d. We know that 10% of our calls to our database equal appointments. This means for me to schedule 24 appointments, I need to talk to 240 people.

e. We know that to talk to 240 people which are 33% of our calls we make, we need to call 720 people in a month. This equates to 36 dials per day based on a 20 day work month.

f. So if an Agent makes 36 dials per day and talks to 12 people per day they will set 1.2 appointments per day resulting in 24 schedule appointments, 12 people showing per month and 4 sales. It's all basic math and it all works!

4. Now that you have your numbers in your head, you need to set up an action plan. You need to talk to 12 people per day so how are you going to do that? Who are you going to call? In reality, 36 dials and talking to 12 people is about 4-6 hours of work. Can you do this every day? Do things get in the way? Sure, they do. Do you have to do 36 dials in one sitting? Not at all. Do a couple hours in the morning, an hour in the afternoon and another couple hours in the evening. Take three days per week and devote them to 8 hours of calling. You only have to dial the phone 180 times to talk to 60 people per week. I don't care how you plan your day just make sure that prospecting is part of your plan.

5. Plan how many Buyers you want to work with verses Sellers. The key to success in this business is having a good mix of both Buyers and Sellers. If you have 25 Buyers and 25 sold listings in a year, there are

your 50 sales. So is this easier said than doing it? Maybe. As I have said, if it were easy there would be a lot of successful Realtors in the country. The reason 90% or more of the Realtors in our country don't succeed is because they do not run their business like a business. They do not spend 80% of their time generating business; they spend 10% or less and wonder why Suzie down the street is selling 4 homes per month. I guarantee you that Suzie down the street is structured or at least more structured than the Realtor sitting by the phone waiting for it to ring!

I'm working on possibly adding a coaching aspect to The Real Estate Success Network. I don't know that I want to take this on. If I do, it's a large commitment on my part. I know that many of you need someone you can talk to once a week and that will hold your head to the fire. Heck, I need that too on the things that I work on! We all do. If you are interested in possibly doing this, please drop me a note and we can discuss. I haven't worked out any details on it yet, but I'm thinking I could handle 5-10 people at a time. In the end, if you are unable to get yourself to make these commitments, then you need someone who is going to make you accountable. That is all a coach is really for. They are not there to tell you how to do everything, they are there to discuss your strategies, help plan your goals and then make sure you do what you say you are going to do.

Now it's time for you to get to work! Go for it!

Chapter Forty-Five: 20 Common Mistakes I See Realtors Make

1. Over-thinking the situation

2. Telling the customer so much that they become terrified of buying a home

3. Lack of work ethic - What are you doing to grow your business?

4. Lack of follow up - If you don't follow up, someone else will

5. Lack of strategy – Don't be a tour guide; help them buy a home

6. Lack of taking control of their customer

7. Saying things in the wrong manner – It's not what you say, it's how you say it

8. Making the customer feel you are there for a check and not to help them.

9. Not asking their customer what is most important to them

10. Not doing what it takes to be successful - This business isn't hard, but it takes dedication and commitment

11. Don't ask the proper questions to find out their customers real needs

12. Don't practice - How many contracts and listing agreements have you written before you have met with customer

13. Lack of preparation - What sets you apart from everyone else? Did you prepare for your

appointments or did you just "show up"?

14. Unprofessional - How did you dress for your appointment? Do you realize that when you dress professionally, people take you more seriously?

15. Don't believe - If you don't believe in yourself, who will?

16. No Humor - The best thing you can do is allow humor into your business. I've made a living off having fun with my customers. The more fun you have with your customers the greater the chance they will tell all their friends about you, not to mention the less stressful the transaction will be. Have fun and enjoy yourself!

17. Spending too much time with buyers that aren't buying and sellers who are unrealistic in pricing

18. Standards - If your standards aren't high enough, you can never break through. Create your standards and create your success. If your standards are to make $30,000 a year that's all you will make.

19. Mindset - You can control everything with your thoughts. "Whether you think you can or think you can't.....you are right!" (Henry Ford)

20. Give Back - The universe works in interesting ways. It rewards those who commit themselves to being a good person and helping others.

So let's look at some of these items in greater detail:

1. Over-thinking the situation - I see many Agents so worried about making a mistake that they never do anything. Keep it simple. This isn't rocket science. It's buying and selling a home.

2. Scaring the customer - Instead of telling the Buyer everything that could possibly go wrong, tell them everything good thing that will go right. Negativity brings on negativity and, likewise, positivity brings on positivity. If you wish bad things on the transaction, you will get them. In the meantime, your customer loses all confidence in you as their Realtor.

3. Lack of Work Ethic - The one thing that separates successful Agents from unsuccessful Agents is work ethic. If you aren't putting 40-50 honest hours a week into this business, there is no reason to be in this business. Go to work everyday with the mindset that you have invested all your money – your life savings – into this business. You will find yourself doing things much differently.

4. Lack of Follow up - The number 1 killer of building a relationship is not doing what you say you are going to do. If you show property to someone and never call them again, do you think they will remain loyal? If you talked to a lead once and never called again, do you think they will remain loyal? If you sold a home and years go by without a peep from you, do you think they will remain loyal? Follow-up will build a customer for life. Referrals are awesome!

5. Lack of Strategy - Do you take the list of properties your customer sends and then just show them the homes on their list? Take the time to look at what they are sending you and find better homes in the same price range. Show the best house second-to-last. Understand your customer's needs and desires. Without a strategy, you are just a tour guide.

6. Lack of Taking Control of your Customer - Who runs the process? Does your customer control everything you do? Did you set the ground rules from the moment you met? If you don't control the process and the transaction, your customer will run all over you and then leave because they don't respect you.

7. Saying things in the wrong manner – It's important to say everything so there's no confusion, but you have to remember that it's about your customer. For instance, saying "You aren't buying right now so I'm only going to show you three houses," vs "What I would really like to do this weekend is show you the different areas in our county so you can decide where you want to live. That's the most important thing. We will still look at some houses, but you have to keep in mind that these particular houses will not be available when you are ready to buy. Then I want you to spend the weekend enjoying Brevard County and everything it has to offer." I said the same thing in both scenarios ("I only want to show them three houses"), but I made my wording all about the Buyer.

8. Making the customer feel it's about the paycheck - Are you rushing through the process? Are you not developing a relationship that can last for years? Are you pushing your Buyer to make an offer? If the customer feels you are only in the deal for the buck, you will never create customers for life. The customer has to feel that they are the most important thing going on in your life at the moment. They want your full attention. This means no answering your phone, checking emails, or texting when you're with a Buyer.

9. Not asking the customer what's most important to them - How can you help your customer accomplish their goals if you don't really understand their goals? The best question you can ask is, "What is most important to you?" Your Buyer will believe you actually care about them and you will now know exactly what you have to do to earn their business.

10. Not doing what it takes to be successful - Do you really work a full day? Do you get up in the morning with a plan to implement? Do you spend most of your day coming up with things to do that don't generate business? If you aren't willing to do whatever it takes, including calling your leads, following-up with customers, doing open houses, reading books to better yourself, volunteering, joining groups, attending fundraisers and knocking on doors, then this is the wrong business for you. Nobody is going to show up at your door and ask you to sell them a house. If you invested $100,000 to start this business, what would you do differently? The answer is usually the same: everything!

11. Don't ask the right questions - Do you ask your Buyer questions? Do you find out your customers' true needs and "Must Haves"? Do you find out their motivation for buying or selling? If you don't ask enough questions, you won't have enough information to do a great job. The more you ask, the more you know, and the more you know, the more sales you get.

12. Agents Don't Practice - How many times have you sat in front of a mirror and practiced a listing presentation or a buyer presentation? How many listing agreements and contracts have you practiced writing so you know them inside and out? Think about most everything you have done in your life whether it is related to sports or music or whatever talent you have worked to cultivate and fine tune. You became good at this talent or skill by practicing. If you don't know your tools of the trade like the back of your hand, you are setting yourself up for failure. You MUST know how to do contracts, listings agreements, buyer brokerage agreements, and both buyer and seller presentations.

13. Lack of Preparation - What do you do to get ready to show property or go on a listing appointment? Do you learn about the area? Do you find out who developed the neighborhood and if the builder was good? Do you know what amenities go with the condo complex or neighborhood? The Boy Scouts said it best, Be Prepared!

14. Unprofessional - How you appear to others is how successful you will be perceived by your customers. If you are meeting a customer for the first time – and I don't care if you are in a beach community or a metropolitan area – you should always dress professionally. First impressions are going to make or break you in this business. If you dress like a slouch, the customer won't take you seriously. I dress in a suit when I meet someone for the first time. It immediately shows the customer that I'm a professional and I take what I do seriously. Your image is extremely important to your success. Shorts and a tee-shirt with sandals won't promote too much confidence in your customer.

15. Don't believe - One of the most important failures of Realtors is their inability to believe in themselves. Think about it. Would you want to work with someone who has a ton of confidence or with someone who is timid and doesn't believe they should be successful? My guess is that half the Agents in the business don't believe they should make $100,000 or more a year. If you don't believe you can do it, you will never do it!

16. No Humor - You don't have to be a comedian, although it would help. You simply have to smile. If you aren't smiling, your customer isn't going to want to spend time with you. Let's face it, buying or selling a home is tough enough; if you aren't enjoying yourself, there is no reason to be doing this. I often look at Agents and they look to me like they are in pain all the time. The hardest thing some Agents should be doing is to look in the mirror and honestly tell themselves that this isn't the career for them. If you genuinely have a great time, smile a lot, and inject humor into the process, everyone has more fun. The number one reason I get 20+ referrals a year, still to this day, is that I had a great time with my customers and they didn't forget it. Looking for a house wasn't a chore, it was a ball!

17. Spending too much time with people who aren't buying or selling - Some Buyers (not *really* Buyers) find it fun to go on vacation and **pretend** they are on HGTV. They go looking at houses and have no problem wasting a day or two of your time while telling you they are planning to buy. If you are working with a Buyer and they are not willing to get pre-approved after you spent a few hours with them, they are not really buying. If your Seller says, "We know it's not worth this much, but we just want to see if we can get it,"...RUN! Don't waste another second with people who aren't really buying or selling. In so doing, you will be taking away precious time you could have spent with serious Buyers or Sellers.

18. Standards - If you have low standards of yourself, you will never break through the glass ceiling. What is the difference between someone who is successful and someone who isn't? Yes, work ethic is most of it, but it's also the standards that you set for yourself. Do you gravitate to low end Buyers? Why? Because it's the standard you feel more comfortable in. Stop it! Get out of your comfort zone and increase your standards.

19. Mindset - You have complete control of your destiny. If you are convinced you can't do this, it's because of your mindset. You CAN do this, but only if you put yourself in the right mindset. I often look at people in general and wonder why they don't accomplish their goals and dreams. It's almost always about their mindset. It controls everything. If you have a negative mindset, then everything in your life will be negative. If you have a positive mindset, everything seems to fall into place. The first step is creating a mantra that becomes ingrained in your brain. There is actual science behind this with regard to neurons and axons, but we'll save that for another manual.

20. Give Back – Working in the field of Real Estate allows you opportunities to give back. Life is all about giving back. Our role in this world is to help others who are less fortunate or who need our help for various reasons. I'm a huge believer in Karma and the Universe. Live your life as a good person. Have sincere honest thoughts. Truly try to help anyone and everyone you can. Make a positive difference in someone else's life every day. Get out of the "it's all about me" role and get into the "what can I do to help?" role, and you will see your life change in so many ways.

I'm sure as you read through this section, if you read it honestly, you have been made aware that you fall into a few or even several of these categories. The good news is you can change if you truly want to. It doesn't make you a bad person to find youself in one of these pitfalls. You have just stepped off the right track and needed someone else to point these things out. The rest is up to you.

Becoming successful in whatever you do in life takes hard work and commitment. If you don't commit, it's very hard to accomplish anything. You have to dive into this with passion and resolve that you ARE going to become very successful, and you ARE going to be the best you can be. Continue to tell yourself that you deserve to be successful.

When you are self-employed, which you are, you are the only person that is going to honestly keep you accountable. It's not easy. If it were, everyone would be doing it successfully. However, you have it in you to accomplish what you want to accomplish. We all do. Sometimes you just need to get out of your own way, to stop thinking about the past, and to really push yourself toward the future. As I've said before, being a Realtor isn't rocket science. It's really one of the easiest professions I've had in my life. But without honest commitment and work ethic, it can be the most difficult career you'll ever face. Smile, have fun, enjoy your customers, be smart, work hard, and most of all care about your customers, your fellow agents, and your community. The world is waiting for you!

Chapter Forty-Six: I Don't Sell You! I Help You!

Well here I am, 53 years old and I finally realize that I understand what it's all about. I believe that most of what I have to say relates to everyday life. It's all about how I choose to live my life and how I teach my children, my staff and basically anyone else who will listen. Lately I have been doing motivational speeches to spread my message. As you read through the final section of this manual, remember that it comes from my heart and soul. It was written with 25 years of hard work with virtually no education, except what I learned on my own.

You have the power in you to succeed at whatever you desire. **Just do it!**

Leads

How can you generate leads? This is an open-ended question. There are so many means of marketing that I can't begin to get into here. That will be another manual. Generating leads usually comes in the form of marketing. Marketing can be as simple as saying hello to someone in the grocery store to as elaborate as a multi million-dollar TV campaign. My favorite is the Internet. If you work the Internet and have an effective website, then collecting leads is extremely easy.

Keep in mind that lead generation is not free. The key is to figure out the most cost-effective means for you to generate leads to build your business.

There is one note I must give you on advertising. I have spent millions of dollars on advertising over the years. During that time period, I always believed I knew what I was doing. Then in 2005 I realized I was wrong. Yes even I can be wrong! I realized that most of my advertising was geared toward name recognition. I would advertise on TV and in the newspaper and send blanket post card mailings all over the place with no consistency. I know the facts: a person needs to see your ad at least 5 times to even remember your product. However, I didn't do a great job of this. I still had my core marketing, my direct response marketing, which worked very well for my companies. So why did I spend all this money working on marketing that didn't work? Some of it might have been ego. It's always fun to see your face in the paper or on TV. Some of it might have been because I didn't really understand what I was doing. Like I said, several years ago it hit me that even with a wealth of knowledge and advertising experience, I wasn't doing it right. Now don't get me wrong. If you have plenty of money to spend, there is nothing wrong with branding and creating a great image. Look at the amount of money big businesses spend. Once you create a large amount of advertising cash, you can spend much more. However, if you are on a budget, then keep your marketing to programs that are going to create leads. Name recognition is a wonderful thing. Generating quality leads at an affordable price is even better!

Follow Up

Have you ever wondered what truly sets aside the successful from the unsuccessful? Don't get me wrong; you can succeed without good follow up.

However, you can't be the best you can be, and you certainly will work harder in order to accomplish your sales goals.

Remember, follow up is important in every aspect of the sale as well as after the sale. If you follow these simple rules, you will see a huge difference. I prefer follow up through email if at all possible. If not, use the old-fashioned post office.

1. **After you talk to clients on the phone for the first time, prior to meeting.** Send along an email letting them know it was great talking to them and you are looking forward to helping them.

2. **Once you have met with the client**. Send them another email letting them know that you appreciate them giving you the time to present your product or service, and that you will get back to them as soon as possible with the answers to their questions…and you look forward to helping them.

3. **Once they have bought from you**. Send them a letter thanking them for using your services. Ask them if they know of anyone else that could use your services and to please refer them to you. This letter should also include a survey form asking them to evaluate your services. Let them know that you are always trying to improve your business, and to please be honest with their answers. The last question should be, "Would you refer me to a friend or business associate?" If yes, then, "Do you know of anyone currently needing my service?" and include spaces for him or her to write in names.

4. **From here on in, keep them on your mailing list**. I'm a big believer in newsletters that can be sent monthly. This allows you to keep your name in front of them forever. By sending them a monthly letter, you are almost guaranteeing that if they need

your services in the future, they will be calling you.

Follow up is the most underused tool in all sales, as well as in our personal lives.

If you are cultivating a new customer, it is imperative to follow up and keep in contact with your customer. There is always someone waiting in line to help him or her if you don't. If you don't follow up, you might as well just give your customer to your competitor. In this day and age you need to stand out and show why your customer is important to you.

All my follow up notes let them know how I look forward to helping them. You will see that if your true intention is to help your customer, your friend, your family or anyone else, you will get rewarded in the end. It may be a sale, a favor, a smile, a hug, or respect. You will always win if you are honestly trying to help. I have repeated myself here, I'm sure!

To follow up correctly, you need a follow up system. There are hundreds of tools out there in the marketplace to help you perform follow up. Many of them are database programs such as Outlook and Act. There are also many companies that offer follow up systems such as monthly post card mailings, monthly newsletter mailings and emailing services. These are all great ways to maintain contact with your database. However, if you collect email addresses, and you should for everyone you meet, then you can do this yourself through your email program on your home computer. Be aware though that if your database becomes too big, your ISP may limit your outgoing mail. If you get to that size, then it becomes worth the investment to purchase your own server and host your own email system. At that point you have no limit to your emailing and you can grow your database as large as you would like. I currently have over 18,000 people in my active database. When I am ready to do my monthly mailing I simply write my note, add a link to my newsletter and press a button. The entire mailing takes about 20 minutes to go out. Once the mailing goes out, the emails start coming in with inquiries. It's almost automatic.

We have mostly talked about follow up with a customer once he or she becomes a customer. What about when you are first starting to talk with a lead? Again, you can use most of the computer programs out there to help you keep organized in your lead follow up. At the beginning of each month, I take all the leads out of the month we are in and file them in the dates I should be calling--simple! Just remember that follow up, as well as follow through, are two of the most important aspect of being successful. If you only do this aspect well, you will have more sales than you have ever had.

Keep in mind that it is so much easier to get an additional sale from a past customer than it is to cultivate a new customer. Most sales people work for the sale and forget that after the sale, follow up is vital. If you have been in business for many years and you haven't been in touch with all your past customers, you are leaving money on the table. I guarantee that one of them or someone they know is ready to buy something that you sell. If you don't keep in touch with them, then they won't buy from you.

I'll finish this section with a story about my brother. My brother Jeff and I are very close. When I first got into the Real Estate business he told me about his Realtor. I said to him, "Jeff, you have lived in your house for years and have no intention on leaving." He said, "You are right, but if I ever do, I am calling my Realtor." So why does my brother have this loyalty to someone who has never sold him a house? About 10 years ago my brother and his wife were thinking about buying a new house. They met a Realtor and he showed them several houses. At that point they decided not to buy. For the past 10 years, my brother and his wife have received birthday cards, anniversary cards and holiday cards.

This is awesome follow up. This Realtor is doing what he should. He is following up even though he never received a sale. Eventually, my brother will move; eventually, he will use this Realtor. Never give up on your customers until they tell you to stop following up. They will appreciate it as well and tell others about you.

The Soft Close

I have read a lot of sales books and frankly don't agree with most of them. Most of them talk about closing techniques and all this other stuff they believe are vital to making sales. I can honestly say that I have never used any of their techniques, at least not consciously. I was never comfortable with selling people. I was always comfortable with helping them.

One might think that I am going to spend a significant amount of time and details dealing with "the close." That is not my plan. Instead, I believe that if you truly believe in your product, and you are truly trying to help your customer, then the sales part of the job is easy. There are some very basic elements that you do need to know to accomplish the goal of helping your customer. First, you have to identify their needs. I know that sounds basic but you would be amazed how many salespeople don't use the easiest sales tool available to them--their ears. So how do you go about identifying their needs? Ok, again this isn't rocket science. To identify their needs, you must ask…questions! However, you must ask the right kind of questions--open-ended questions.

Open-ended questions are questions that cannot be answered with one word. They can't be answered with a simple yes or no. Open-ended questions allow your customer to elaborate on his or her needs. By using these types of questions, you are able to obtain a substantial amount of information, which, in turn, will give you the tools to **help your customer**. I know I have said this before and I am sure I will say this many more times: Help your customer. Help your customer. Help your customer. If you help your customer, you will get paid. It's really that simple. An open-ended question can be as simple as, "How can you see (insert product) helping you to (do whatever)?" Simple questions like this will let customers sell themselves on the product. Once they sell themselves, they are really buying you and your company. For this reason, it is important that they trust and believe in your knowledge of the industry and products. You need to show the ability to understand their business.

Okay, I know you have been waiting for the powerful question that is going to change your sales life. I know that all top sales people must have something in common. There must be many ways to maneuver your customer into buying your product or service. Are you ready? The answer to this age-old dilemma is so simple you are not going to believe me. Okay, here it is…**Ask for the Sale**. That's it. That is the secret between being good and being mediocre. You have to ask for the sale. That is the powerful close, which has allowed me to reach the top sales position in every company I have either worked for or owned. I have seen so many sales people go into a situation and do a terrific job of educating and answering objections and questions. They know their product, they are honest, they are well-liked, well-groomed and have great work ethics, but they still don't get the sale. The reason is they don't ask for the sale. I know what you are saying. It can't be that easy. But it is.

One exercise that I have used most of my life to help me become the best sales person I can be is to reverse roles. I always ask myself, what would I want? How would I like to be treated? What would make me buy this product? For some reason people don't always put those ingredients together. People don't always treat people the way they want to be treated. I use this technique in many aspects of both my personal and business life. I find that by reversing roles I am able to really understand my customers better.

So the "soft close" is truly soft. There is no pressure involved. Not only will you receive a tremendous amount of new sales from this easy technique, you will find that your referral rate climbs through the roof. You will also find that your customers will become repeat customers. The two most important aspects of sales are repeat customers and referrals. As I have said, it is much easier to develop a current or past customer versus trying to build a new customer. At this point I have been in Real Estate for over 13 years.

When I first started, I employed everything that I talk about in this manual. I gave my customers great customer service, lots of hard work and attention and, most important, I truly cared about my customers and they knew it. I worked my tail off the first couple of years building my business. Fast-forward a couple of years. Even though we generate over 30 - 60 buyer leads per day, I do not need to take any of these leads to have a very successful Real Estate career. The reason for this is everything that I am trying to get through to you. I provided excellent service with great work ethic, great follow up and I truly cared about my customers. For that reason, I continually receive referrals and business from many of my past customers. I remain the top Agent in my company and I don't even sell Real Estate anymore.

This is all done because of the groundwork I have laid while building my business.

If you got nothing out of this manual, please take with you that if you **help your customer and ask for the sale**, you will succeed more than your wildest dreams would have ever believed.

Don't for a second believe that the soft sales approach doesn't mean you don't have to work hard. You will always have to work hard to succeed; the difference is as you start to succeed, you will learn more and more about working smart.

Working hard and working smart doesn't always mean you have to work long hours. I know many successful people that work only 30-50 hours per week. I can tell you that when they first started that was not the case. They worked very hard and very long hours to accomplish their goals. They also spent a lot of time learning and educating themselves in their industry. The more you understand, the easier it is to build. This is all done through time management and systems.

Building Your Business

I have always looked at each job I have had as if it were my own business. I don't know how to do a half ass job at anything. I either do it right or I don't do it at all. More important than money is the fact that I have done a great job and have been the best I can be. Money always follows success.

One of the commonest mistakes I see small business people making is not having a plan. Without a plan you can't have future goals or means to accomplish those goals. I have learned a lot over the years and I am going to recap a few of the most important aspects of building a business.

First, to build a business you must have a written plan. The plan must incorporate 1 – 5 years of financial goals. The plan must have a marketing plan to understand how you are going to obtain your financial goals. This plan is always a work in progress. Nothing is as easy as it seems when you write it down. However, everything is obtainable if you do write these goals and plans down. I have written many business plans. Some are very elaborate and some are just a couple of pages.

The key is to write down and follow the plan. When something isn't working you have to deviate, and then just add the changes to the plan. I don't think I have ever followed my plan exactly the way it was written because in business, things change all the time. Once you really get into the nuts and bolts of running your business you will see that there are many things that you thought you knew in which you really didn't know.

It's just reality.

I was talking to my friend Mike just the other day. Mike is a great guy and one of my best friends. We met when we were 15 years old. That's 32 years ago. Amazing!

Mike truly has a great heart and is always thinking about helping people. He has been there when I have done well and he has always been the first person there when I fell down. His words of encouragement are very honest and sincere. He will always hold a strong place in my heart. Mike has been very successful in land development. He currently owns shopping plazas in the Northeast. This past year Mike has decided to venture into a new business, a golf range-training facility and restaurant. When we talked the other day we had a great discussion about how much more involved this work was than building shopping centers. Everything he thought he had planned was set to go. Of course, there was something else that came up that either cost more money or had him adjusting his plan. The reason I am telling you this is to understand that no matter how successful you are or have been in the past, you will always find things are not as easy as when you first came up with the concept. **Be prepared to adjust and go with the flow**.

The other thing that Mike and I talked about is systems, one of the most important aspects of running a business. Systems are so important that the lack of systems are the reason that **over 90% of startup businesses fail**. Most people start a business with little or no business experience. They were good in their job and now they want to own their own company. I applaud them for wanting to make this move. They are on their way to the biggest adventure of their lives. But if you are going to take the risk, do it right.

Without systems you have no way of growing your business. The reason we use systems is to be able to have documented procedures on how we run our businesses. Every business should have an operations manual. During your business life you will be hiring, firing, training and retraining people. You will have great people and you will have not so great people. You will hire people you thought were going to be awesome that turned out to be busts and vice versa. If you have systems, you will be able to plug most anyone into the system and it will work. Look at McDonalds. They have done this better than anyone. They knew that to operate a very profitable business they must have simple documented means of accomplishing all the tasks that are needed to run a McDonalds. They also did this for duplication purposes. You can go into a McDonalds in Massachusetts or a McDonalds in Florida and you will find they are exactly the same. Systems.

(Read Michael Gerber's *E-Myth* – This book changed how I look at running businesses and to me is the best book on business.)

Most businesses get started without systems and then add them later. This is doable but definitely not the smartest way to get going. I have done it both ways and can tell you that having great systems in place will accomplish a heck of a lot more for you in a much shorter time period. There are many systems that go into running a business. Here is a list of some of them.

Systems

1. Accounting
2. Marketing Systems
3. Lead Generation
4. Lead Delegation and Distribution
5. Lead Follow Up
6. Customer Follow Up
7. Phone Answering Procedures
8. Sales Calls
9. Customer Support
10. Sales Support
11. Inventory
12. Pricing
13. Commission
14. Paperwork
15. Management
16. Training
17. Recruiting
18. Firing

There are so many more possible systems; it all depends on the type of business you open. These are just a few to give you an idea of what you need to do when you get started. These all must be in writing because if it isn't written it isn't law.

You should also have your job descriptions written and given to your employees as you hire them. It is important that they understand exactly what they are expected to do at a minimum. Of course my favorite line at the bottom of each job description reads something like this: "These are your duties along with anything else you may come up with in the course of doing business which needs your attention." This lets them know that they need to adjust with the flow as things change. In other words, job descriptions may be changed as needed.

The other major reason we build systems is for growth. To grow smoothly, we need to be able to duplicate our efforts. If our systems are in writing, this growth becomes much easier to control and obtain. One of the flaws I see in small businesses that want to grow is that they try to go too big too quickly. I'm a believer in slow, steady growth. Growth shouldn't start until you have all your systems in place and understand your business totally. In my opinion, the first year of business is a learning curve. This is when you find out that things aren't exactly what you had thought they were and changes are needed.

I like growing from the inside out. I have always been one to promote from within. Usually, when I start a company I have someone in mind to take over my position as soon as possible. Remember, you want the business to work for you, not you work for the business. It took me years to figure that one out. By having someone groomed to take over, when you are ready to move on, the transition is easier. Easy is good.

When you start to grow your business think compact. Grow your business slowly and surely at first. After you have your business running smoothly and successfully you can think about opening another office, location, branch or adding markets. The key to growth is to take your time and do it right. Don't be in such a hurry to be rich. If you take your time your odds increase tremendously. Just add one location at a time and when it is up and running as smoothly and successfully as your first, go to the next.

I also believe in building out with your business. To me this only makes sense. Why add a location that is not close to your original location? Until you have mastered opening locations, be sure that your new location is close enough for you to be there quickly in case of an emergency. As you start to grow this way you can eventually hire regional management to help you maintain and grow your locations while you spend time expanding. If you grow smart, you will increase your chances of being successful.

The Power of Free

I like free! **Free is a great thing that most small businesses do not take advantage of or understand.** I have told this to many people and they look at me strangely. They say, "I can't afford to do that. That will cost me a fortune."

Next door to my office is a pizza place. They have excellent pizza, probably the best in the area. Unfortunately, the owner struggled greatly with his restaurant. At one point he asked me what he could do to get the message out about his pizza and to get more people through his door. The first question I asked him was how much it cost to make a pizza. He told me it cost him about $2. That means it probably cost him closer to $1.50 or so.

I said to him, "Why don't you give away pizza on National Pizza Day?" His answer to me of course was that there is no such thing as NPD. I said that he was right, but why not start one? He thought the idea was silly and didn't want to spend the money. But think about it. All he had to do was send a mailing to 1,000 homes advertising free pizza on National Pizza Day. Just stop by the pizza place and get your one free pizza with this coupon. My guess if he sent 1,000 coupons out, he would have had close to two or three hundred redemptions. Ok, so let's look at the costs; if it cost him $2 for a pizza and he gave away 300 pizzas, the cost would be $600. To do a post card mailing to 1,000 homes cost about $400. So for $1,000 he would have received 200-300 new customers that would have loved his pizza because it was great pizza. Not to mention that if they came in the door they were likely to buy another pizza or a drink or something else because they were getting the free pizza. He most likely would have made his money back from other sales with his new customer base. Don't you think they would have told everyone about their free pizza no strings attached? If you run an ad in the paper for $500 and get only 10 customers you are pretty happy. **Can you see the power of free**?

Unfortunately, he is now out of business. If he had only listened to me I guarantee you he would still be in business and business would be thriving. He is a great example of those who want and talk about success, but don't do anything about it.

This process is very cost effective and is a great way, probably the best way, to insure a quick start to your business. People will always respond to free stuff. Our society loves it. The best way to see if this works for you is to simply figure out the cost of acquiring a sale. Once you know the cost of acquiring a sale you can determine if giving away product will be the best way of building your client base.

Now here is another example of the power of free.

My last company was called Internet Community Concepts. We worked with radio and TV groups developing private label Internet products. Of course that wasn't a product you could give away so I had to come up with something better.

To be successful, I had to get meetings with the top radio executives in the country. My brain started going and I realized that most executives play golf. That was the answer. I knew there were 12 executives I wanted to meet. I quickly ordered 12 putters, 12 putting greens for the office and a dozen golf balls. Everything had our ICC logo on it. I then sent all these Next Day Mail to the executives with a note that said, "While you are putting around trying to figure out your next Internet move, give ICC a call and let us help." It was simple and to the point. This giveaway got me in contact with 6 of the 12 executives I wanted to meet. I got half my goal with a simple and relatively inexpensive marketing approach. They were very welcoming when I called and I worked with a few of them regularly. Even though my company ran out of money prior to me securing any deals with these six, I had job offers from a few of them when my company closed down. (The company was sold for $80 million, but the deal fell apart right after the stock market crashed in April of 2000.) If I had more time, I would have converted a couple of them to customers. The radio world was very slow to react to the Internet. However I did get the name Mr. Internet in Radio Inc. magazine and was a guest speaker at several conferences. I learned a lot during that time period.

Again, the power of free is very successful.

Building Long Term Relationships
Many businesses and sales people go after the

quick buck. This is a big mistake. To be successful in business it is imperative that you build successful relationships with your customers. They will be the lifeblood of any business you choose to start. I have seen so many businesses and sales people that go after the quick buck and end up being big losers in the long run.

I recently had my pool resurfaced at my house as well as my dock rebuilt. Now here is a great example of two companies working with two completely different objectives in mind. Let's start with the pool company. We went into the pool company and they were as nice as can be. The owner as well as their sales rep spent a substantial amount of time talking to us and discussing our options. Both my wife and I felt comfortable with the company and the owner. We went ahead with the job and gave them the deposit. This was in July. The owner assured me that the pool would take no more than a week to two weeks once they got started.

They were to start two weeks later. Of course, once they had our deposit we were kind of stuck. Sound familiar? They didn't start working on our pool for almost two months after we had signed on the dotted line. They gave us tons of excuses why they were behind, the main one being that other jobs ahead of ours were taking longer to finish. Oh yes, I forgot to mention that they had drained our pool at the two week mark so during this time period we couldn't use our pool at all. Once they started working on the pool we were excited about finally being able to use it even though by then it was the end of summer. Well, the one to two weeks they promised at signing turned into over two months.

It was ridiculous. They came out and worked on the pool for an hour here and an hour there. The owner wouldn't really talk to us anymore and the sales rep blamed this guy or that one. Well, it finally was finished and looked great. No problem at all with the work. It was beautiful. Within a week, we noticed that the waterfall was leaking. To make a very long story short, it took 4 months for them to fix the leak. I finally threatened to take them to court to get the money back so I could hire someone else to get the waterfall fixed. I must have called them 15 times without ever getting a call back.

I went into the store several times until they just got sick of me and fixed the thing. So to recap, they didn't deliver what they said they would do and they would not respond or return my calls when I wanted answers. This is a perfect example of a take-the-money-and-run attitude we have all experienced so many times from businesses and sales people. Being in the Real Estate business we often get asked for recommendations for pool companies. If this company had done right by me they would have had at least 5 referrals by now. The reality is that I have told many people that they were terrible and advised them not to buy from them. There's an old saying: if you do a great job they will tell 5 people and if you do a bad job they will tell 20 people.

Let's move forward to the dock company. I called three companies to come out to my house for a quote. I decided on the person who actually came in higher in price than the other two. I did this because I felt good about the person, and I had talked to a couple of people that had used him and said he was great. We had a hurricane and so he ended up starting the job a month and a half later than we contracted. The difference between the Pool Company and the Dock Company in dealing with this was amazing. The dock guy called me weekly to update me on the status of when he was going to get to my dock. He always thanked me for being patient.

He threw in a better boatlift because he appreciated my patience. I never had to call him to find out when he would be there because he called me first. Once he started, he told me that it would take 3 weeks to complete. It actually took 4 weeks because he felt that the sea wall needed some work, and he didn't charge me extra. He said that the most important aspect of his work was to make sure his customer was happy. He, the owner, was always available when I had a question and still is when I have called him a few times with questions. In the meantime, I have referred 3 people to him so far and will always recommend him to my customers. On a side note, after almost 4 years, he recently came out to my house within a few days of a call and fixed a sinking staircase. Of course, there was no charge.

So why am I telling you all this? The pool guy was going for the quick buck. Eventually, this will come back to bite him. Eventually, all the people that he made the quick buck from will tell enough people, and his business will go down. When the market slows down, so will his business.

The dock guy, on the other hand, made a conscious effort to keep us informed and explained everything. He earned our business for life. When I have a customer that needs dock work, I gladly give them AJ's phone number.

When you are building your business, be sure to follow the dock guy's method of dealing with issues. There are always circumstances that come up that might delay your delivery. Things happen all the time. If you treat your customers like gold, you will get a great return on your investment. You can never go wrong by keeping your customers informed. **Build your business relationships for life and you will have a life-long business.**

If you remember, we talked about a follow up system. Again, and I can't say this enough, it is so much less expensive to keep a past customer and receive additional business from them than it is to find new business. If you do a great job and continue to keep in contact with them after the sale, you will have a customer for life. Just think. The next time you have a new product to market you can simply contact your current customer base to start the sales process. They already trust you and will buy from you again because you did what you said you were going to do, and didn't go after the quick buck. I like contacting past customers a minimum of 4 times per year. We do this in newsletters, holiday cards and 'just saying hi' emails. This is very simple and all very inexpensive.

Help As Many People As Possible

This last portion of my manual is really the most important part of my philosophy. It is not my philosophy alone but that of almost every successful person I have ever met or read about. It's all about giving back and helping people.

I spend probably as much time thinking about

how I can help people as I do thinking about how I can make my company successful. The theory is that **good things happen to good people.** This is so true. I know that it might be hard to believe, but there is so much truth in this statement. I, like most of the successful people I know, try to give 10% of my income back to charity. But it doesn't stop at money. It's about getting involved and doing something to make my community a better place to live.

When I was a kid, probably 16 or so, I remember seeing some inner city kids causing trouble in Boston. I started thinking then about how we could change this attitude. I learned that there were so many young kids dropping out of school and turning to a life of crime. I knew there was a way to help them, but I wasn't sure how. Well, now I do. I, along with a couple of other wonderful people, have started a foundation called Hope Chest. Hope Chest's purpose is to sponsor children and send them to college if they graduate high school. We are just in the beginning of this foundation and it has been a ton of work to get going. However, the work will pay off in 12 years when we start sending 250 kids a year to college.

These are children that have no hope and, therefore, no dreams. Their idea of success is a drug dealer driving a BMW. By showing them in first grade that they have hope and a chance at success, we are changing families for generations to come. It's awesome and it is my purpose in life. Everything else that I do, I do to support my family and pay my bills. I want to help as many people as possible.

To me, this is the best thing I can do for my community. If all goes well, I will be expanding this program throughout the state of Florida and then throughout the country. After all, education will change lives. When I am on my deathbed, this is how I want to be remembered.

I don't think I can impress upon you how important it is to help your neighbor. By doing so you give yourself an impressive standing in the community, but more importantly it will make you feel good. There is nothing that feels quite as good as knowing you have helped someone. **It's good for business and it's great for the soul!**

There are so many things you can do. I encourage my entire staff to do something to help. I encourage them to volunteer at schools, hospitals, soup kitchens and more. One of my staff members runs a golf tournament for MS each year and is very successful with this event. You can never give enough. Remember, it's not always about money. If you don't have much and can't afford to give any away at this time, find another way to give. Teach your children to give and to help. Start them on the right path to understanding that not everyone has life as good as they do, and that people need help. The only way they truly receive help is from other people.

Chapter Forty-Seven: And in the End

Well, this is the end of my manual. Hopefully, you have gained some insight into how I have become successful and how I have trained many others to be successful too. Life is very short and it's important that you do the best you can and do it with a good heart. Never jeopardize your integrity for a buck. Always try to help your customers accomplish their goals. Always treat people with respect--the way you would like to be treated. These are all just part of the Golden Rules of Life.

In the end, don't forget what is really important in life. Your family will be and should be your highest priority. Even though we talk about how hard you have to work to be successful, don't lose sight of your family. Take time to smell the roses. Be sure to take as many vacations per year as possible. It's important to recharge those batteries and reward yourself for all your hard work. You deserve it.

Don't worry about failing at whatever you decide to do. If you follow most of my guidelines you are increasing your chances for success. However, there are so many circumstances that can affect you both in a positive or negative way. Don't let that deter you from giving 100% to succeed in your dreams. Don't listen to all the people that are going to tell you that you are crazy for thinking about following your dreams. They will tell you that you are being irresponsible. They will tell you that you don't know what you are doing. They will tell you anything to stop you from doing this.

Why? The real reason is that they don't want you to succeed.

If you succeed, that makes it harder for them to accept the fact that they didn't follow their heart and their dreams. Once you start on your way to following your dream, they will fight you every step of the way. They can't wait to tell you, "I told you so." Remember, even if you don't succeed in your first business attempt, you didn't fail. You succeeded in accomplishing what most of the world would love to do, but didn't have the courage to. You might not have succeeded in winning in the business world, but you can certainly go to your grave knowing that you tried and took the risk. You will have no regrets. Think about that…no regrets. If you can go to your death with no regrets then you won at the game of life. That's the goal from the beginning. So in closing, I want you to remember just one final thing. Be honest to yourself, be honest to your customers, be honest to your family and **Just Do It!**

Afterword by Joe Rando

I've have been silent in this blog for a few weeks. There are a number of reasons for this but the main one is that, after an illness, I said goodbye to my father, Tony Rando, last week. These kind of life events have a way of overshadowing everything else, as they should. But as this blog day approached, I realized just how much of my beliefs and attitudes about business came from this man and I couldn't write about anything else. I am not sure if this will be interesting for you but I am positive it will be cathartic for me...

At 28 years old, my father found himself with a wife and a 6 month old son (me). But he also had a family restaurant that had just partially burned and was under-insured. One owner of this restaurant, his uncle, was in the hospital with cancer, and the other owner, his father, was dead at 47 of a heart attack, probably from the shock of the fire. I can't imagine what it must have been like to be in such a desperate situation - having the livelihood of three families on your shoulders when you're not even 30. But my father did what he always

did, meeting the situation with a combination of creativity and sheer grit, focusing on what was most important to achieve a single goal, saving the business. And he succeeded. He used the insurance money to rebuild, getting help from friends and family to stretch the dollars. He talked the vendors into extending credit until he could pay them back and he reimagined the business, making it into a combined restaurant/entertainment venue with live music to pull in the crowds. He saved the business and turned it over to his now recovered uncle.

Then he went off and started his own restaurant, leasing space in a hotel. By his second year he was doing $750,000, which is an insane amount of revenue for a restaurant in those days. In 2015 dollars this is equivalent to $5.8 million. He clearly knew how to run a restaurant. What he didn't know was how important good legal representation was. The people leasing him the space saw how successful it was and used a clause in the lease to take the restaurant back. He never forgot this lesson and use top-notch attoneys from then on.

Eventually the family restaurant was sold and he had some money. What he did with the money from the sale was the most amazing thing. He did absolutely nothing. He didn't invest it, or buy a house, or a better car. He sat on it and waited. He waited until he had a sure winner, a situation where he could buy a dollar for fifty cents. And then he acted decisively, closing a deal in under 48 hours. This was it and he knew it and nothing would stop him.

You see, when the family restaurant was sold, there were some problems and he had to quit his job as the manager of a Holiday Inn to run the family restaurant again for a while. When it was finally sold, he was out of a job. The new manager of the Holiday Inn didn't run it as well and profit was down. Later the owners decided to sell it and the buyers lost one partner at the last minute. My father knew he could make money with this hotel (he already had) and stepped in with the cash, he and the partners buying the property at a discount due to mediocre management.

Since he had the upper hand, his lawyers tried to convince him to take control from the other partners but he adamantly refused saying "I have to work with these people." His partners were good people too and they ran this hotel the way they lived, with great business acumen and compassion for others. This was evident when the unions tried to unionize the hotel and the employees had no interest. They were already treated fairly.

Years later he ended up in the shopping center business and his (and his partners') compassion were regularly evident. Some of the tenants were mom & pops and they were signed personally to their leases. When some of these mom & pops didn't make it, they worked it out, letting them go without penalty. They never forgot that these were people.

I could go on but you get the idea.

While I have an MBA, my most valuable business lessons came from my father. Here are ten of them:

1. ***If you can own real estate, do.*** Most of the value in the restaurant he sold was in the real estate.

2. ***Choose good businesses.*** He came to realize that the restaurant business was tough and moved into hotels, which have higher barriers to entry.

3. ***The Golden Rule applies in business too.*** It is your reputation and relationships with other people that will make all the difference. People liked him and they came to his rescue when the restaurant burned.

4. ***The most sure-fire way to make money is to create value.*** I know this sounds obvious but I came of age during the real estate bubble of the 1980s when everyone was making money by flipping stuff. Tying up land and permitting it was a much safer (though more difficult) way to make a profit. He made sure I knew this.

5. ***Find your focus and work hard on it.*** Otherwise you wind up doing too many things and result in accomplishing nothing.

6. ***Wait for your pitch.*** Don't pursue an opportunity just because you want to do *something*. Wait until there is an opportunity that you can really make into a success.

7. ***Hire top-notch legal counsel.*** This is not a place where you should be bargain hunting. My father learned this the hard way.

8. ***Pay attention to the financial statements.*** Again obvious, but you'd be shocked how many entrepreneurs don't do it.

9. ***You can only wear one pair of pants at a time.*** This was his way of saying not to get enamored with "things." It is a meaningless and soulless existence.

10. ***At the end of the day, all of this is about taking care of your family.*** He made it clear every day that there is nothing more important.

I feel very lucky to have had such a good teacher. And I will miss his counsel for the rest of my life. Thank you for taking the time to learn a bit about this man who had such a positive influence on so many people.

Regards,

Joe Rando

If you enjoyed this book, please take a moment to review it on Amazon for other readers to discover it.

About The Author

Over the years, Mitch has owned several businesses ranging from a paintball company, dating services, internet companies, and finally a real estate firm, where he found his calling in 2001. After creating a unique internet business model, he opened Tropical Realty of Suntree, which has grown from 6 Agents to 70+ agents, 3 locations, and ranked as the #1 Independent Real Estate office in Brevard County with plans to open 1 additional location this year. Mitch's first book, *100MPH Marketing for Real Estate*, peaked at #1 on Amazon for real estate marketing books, and goes hand in hand with the 100MPH marketing software and systems that focus on internet marketing and lead conversion. Brokerages and seminar companies have hired Mitch to speak on the topic for as short as 1-hour, which birthed *Coaching for a Cure*, a way to raise research funds for Sturge Weber Syndrome, a disease his granddaughter, Lola, was born with in 2006. For a $200 donation, Mitch provides 1-hour of coaching with all proceeds benefiting disease research through his charity Lola's Gift ($500 value). Learn more @ www.lolasgift.com & www.facebook.com/coaching4acure. Mitch resides in Merritt Island, Florida, with his wife, Jeanette. Together, they have four children: Jon, Matt, Michael, and Amanda, as well as two amazing grandchildren: Henry and Lola.

About The Editor

Jaimie M. Engle is a freelance writer and President of A Writer For Life in Melbourne, Florida. Her work has appeared in *Writer's Journal Magazine*, on the Dr. Laura program's website, and *Writer's Digest*, plus dozens of other journals, magazines, and newspapers. She writes regularly for *Space Coast Living Magazine*, teaches workshops at colleges, conferences, and libraries, and has assisted many authors to publish and promote their work as well as her own novels. You can read her client's testimonials at www.awriterforlife.com.

71360580R00142

Made in the USA
Columbia, SC
25 May 2017